FROM
PROCRASTINATION TO
PRODUCTION
7 Steps to Change Your Life NOW!

JEFFERY COMBS

Published by
Golden Mastermind Seminars, Inc.

Golden Mastermind Seminars, Inc.

6507 Pacific Avenue #329
Stockton, CA 95207
Toll Free 800-595-6632
FAX: 209-467-3260
www.GoldenMastermind.com

Cover and interior by FlowMotion, Inc.
Editorial services provided by Creative Editorial Solutions

ISBN: 978-1-934919-14-9

Printed in the United States of America

PREFACE

This book is dedicated to procrastinators everywhere: those who suffer from infrequent procrastination as well as chronic procrastinators. For the last twenty-plus years, I have witnessed many quality, capable people with lots of talent sabotage themselves by procrastinating. For more than ten years of my entrepreneurial career, I developed sales teams and sales organizations. I was amazed at how many people put off and/or avoided learning the habits and skills associated with selling. I began to take note of how many of them procrastinated about mastering the sales process, and even quit to avoid the perceived pain associated with selling. This began my journey into understanding the reasons and the science behind why so much of the population procrastinates.

Over thirteen years ago, I started personally mentoring and coaching entrepreneurs, business owners, athletes, entertainers, those with addictions, and individuals from all walks of life. I have since coached over 6,000 clients and devoted 60,000 hours of my personal time to coaching. I have personally witnessed how many people procrastinate. I also found that there is very little written and understood on this topic that affects so much of the population. This book is a handbook based on my practical experience, my research, and my committed study on why we procrastinate. I offer specific methods to assist you to release the causes of procrastination so you will live less frequently in the effects of procrastination.

I provide insight into the six main procrastinator types and their shared commonalities, and I present the techniques and skills to assist you to let go of the events, people, and situations that keep you procrastinating.

In the following pages, you will gain understanding about why you procrastinate and you will learn detailed steps on how to let go. Be patient as you begin to understand your procrastinator type(s) and the reasons why you do what you do. Persevere, because transformation from occasional and chronic procrastination is not an overnight process. You must be committed and serious about letting go of the causes that create and perpetuate your procrastination.

If you are reading this book, you are taking the first steps to become a recovering procrastinator. Congratulations! You deserve to receive the benefits of dropping the procrastinator identity and reinventing yourself to become the person you deserve to be.

With gratitude,
Jeffery Combs

TABLE OF CONTENTS

INTRODUCTION

Before we begin, I have a confession to make right up front: I, Jeffery Combs, the president and founder of Golden Mastermind Seminars, Inc., procrastinated about writing this book. I came up with the idea for this book several years ago when I realized that there was very little content available on the subject of procrastination. Pay a visit to any bookstore in America, and you will be hard-pressed to find books and CDs that specifically focus on procrastination. The reason? Procrastination is a very misunderstood topic – there's very little understanding of how to let go of procrastination, how to recognize and diffuse the feelings that lead to procrastination, and most importantly, how to develop the ability to both produce and relax without guilt.

Procrastination Is an Effect – Not a Cause

We all procrastinate occasionally. Procrastination can be defined as delaying a project, a task, or an intended course of action, despite expecting to feel the guilt or shame of the delay. Fifteen to 20 percent of adults routinely put off activities that would best be accomplished as soon as possible. In independent surveys conducted in 2007, 80–90 percent of all college students admitted that they had major issues with procrastination.

Procrastination is an effect, not a cause. You don't procrastinate because you're a procrastinator. You procrastinate because there are causes that have created the effect of procrastination.

To begin to let go of your procrastination, it's important to understand *why* you procrastinate.

As you cover the material in this book, I would like to introduce you to an important distinction: If you call yourself a procrastinator, this word becomes your identity. No one is a cut-and-dried procrastinator in all areas of their life. Instead, we procrastinate in isolated areas where we perceive pain, we procrastinate to rebel, or we procrastinate to control a situation. Many people who are rebellious in their procrastination often wind up rebelling against their own success. This is taking procrastination to the extreme.

The most common form of procrastination occurs when you fail to adhere to an end result without any passion or reasoning. You create an excuse in order to eliminate the perception of pain. If just thinking about tomorrow's tasks and chores brings up feelings of anxiety, pain, or discomfort, there is a high probability that something more trivial will be created to avoid the pain. You will most likely not schedule less-critical tasks for later. This is the primary reason that you get sidetracked. It's the reason that you plan to make business calls and suddenly find yourself at the refrigerator.

Procrastination Is an Epidemic

Procrastination, quite frankly, is an epidemic, and an epidemic can only be eliminated if the underlying root cause is discovered. My goal for this book is to teach you how to identify what causes procrastination and neutralize the resulting feelings. I'll show you how to go from procrastinator to producer. No matter who you are, this book will assist you to overcome procrastination and achieve the life of your dreams.

1

An Overview
of Procrastination

Early in my entrepreneurial career, I became aware of the prevalent tendency toward procrastination that was built into large sales teams around the country. People would attend my rallies, events, seminars, conventions, trainings, and mastermind groups, and they would leave inspired and excited. Then they would return home, back to their familiar surroundings, and procrastinate rather than produce.

These individuals joined what I call the Witness Protection Program, meaning that they would not return my phone calls or respond to my emails – I would never hear from them again. At first, this used to baffle me; I was shocked at the small number of people that actually followed through on their intentions. They would *intend* to create the action required, but they wouldn't actually *commit*.

Eventually, I learned that this was normal behavior for most of society. A large percentage of the population seeks change, yet these individuals fail to take action because change and success would contradict their struggle. To date in 2010, I have personally coached and mentored around 6,000 individual clients. This adds up to approximately 60,000 personal hours spent mentoring and coaching people to understand the way they feel so they can change those feelings in order to change the way they act. Predictably, 80–90 percent of my clients are stuck in procrastination.

These days, I'm passionate about assisting individuals to understand not only the reason they feel the way they feel but also to recognize the events that created those feelings. If all you do is address the effect, you'll never get to the cause – and the cause is where you learn to live in the solution. If you live in the effect, you'll continue to live in the problem.

Take diet and exercise, for example. If food is a situation that affects you, going on a diet and beginning an exercise program are going to be components of releasing weight. But in the end, they're only the superficial cause that creates the effect. If you first begin to address the reasons you overeat, then you can get to the cause of your procrastination and resistance to weight loss. Many of us start a diet in late December or January, yet somewhere around March and April the luster wears off. We go to the gym in January and February, but the enrollments drop in March and April. The sun comes out, the weather gets nicer, and we lose sight of our goal.

A Short History of Procrastination

Procrastination has been around as long as humans have been in existence. In early societies, a late crop could lead to starvation. Going back to 800 BC, the Greek poet Hesiod equated procrastination with sin or sloth. As society moved into the industrial age, it became easier to procrastinate because machines allowed people to perform less work.

Today, in the era of technology, procrastination is thriving. Not paying attention, getting ready to get ready, surfing the Web, playing computer games, watching the electronic income reducer (i.e., television) are just some of the ways the vast majority of the population avoids doing what they intend to do but are never fully committed to achieving: their dreams, their objectives, and even some of their commitments.

Facebook, Twitter, and other forms of social media have created a whole new way to stay connected – and a whole new way to procrastinate.

"I'm going to prospect on Facebook," you say to yourself. Instead, what happens is that you catch up on all the posts, but you don't do any connecting because you get seduced into avoiding the pain. This is a great example of being busy rather than productive. The seduction of social media allows you to put off what you should do while spending more time doing what you merely want to do. Succumbing to these enticements can absolutely be costly. It can cost you time; it can cost you money. More importantly, it can cause you to experience guilt and shame, the lowest level of feelings that we transmit to others telepathically through our emotional vibrations. Some of the highest levels of feeling that we can vibrate from are love, serenity, and bliss – I believe you can agree that these are challenging emotions to operate from while in the midst of procrastination!

The Financial Costs of Procrastination

Financial experts estimate that 40 percent of our population has experienced a financial loss due to procrastination – and in many cases, the losses were severe. In 2002, America overpaid $473 million in taxes as a result of rushing and creating costly errors. Each year, a large percentage of the population waits until the last minute to file their tax returns. An alarming number of people file extensions and then operate in a panicked rush to meet the extension deadline. Keep in mind that this is in addition to those individuals that completely put off filing taxes altogether and fall years behind.

I once coached a client who hadn't paid taxes in fifteen years. She was so anxious about the repercussions of her situation that she couldn't file her taxes for fear of the unknown, and she was unable to sleep at night. She knew eventually she would have to face the music. Now, this woman wasn't a tax protestor, and it wasn't that she didn't want to pay her taxes. She wasn't dishonest or disloyal to our country. She was simply a chronic procrastinator.

Occasional Procrastinators

There's a huge difference between someone who procrastinates occasionally and someone who procrastinates chronically. We'll cover the chronic procrastinator a little later in this book. For now, I'm going to assume that most of you who are reading this book are occasional procrastinators. You're average procrastinators. You're not addicted to procrastination, but there are areas where procrastination hinders you.

Take a look at your bank account. Does procrastination hinder you there? Take a look at your physique and your health. Does procrastination hold you back you there? Take a look at your desk. Is it piled high with papers that you can't let go of? Is your house a maze of clutter? How about your closet? When you open the door, does everything fall down on you? Or maybe you're one of those people whose garage is so filled with stuff that there's no room for the cars. Now, that's procrastination!

Key Questions to Ask Yourself:

- What is the byproduct of my procrastination?
- Does procrastination cause me guilt and shame?

- Do I feel overwhelmed when it comes to the process of change?
- Do my abandonment and rejection issues keep me from using the electronic income creator (i.e., the telephone)?
- Does procrastination keep me from avoiding production?
- Does the pain of producing hinder me?
- Would producing actually liberate me?

Perfection – or Mastery?

No matter what you do, you will never be 100 percent. This isn't about being 100 percent anything. This isn't about being "the best." This is about being *your* best. You will always have challenges. You will have ups and downs. However, your ability to bounce back will determine whether you are barely in the game or whether you master the game.

You are brilliant. You are already perfect. Your soul is having human experiences. You are exceptional. You have what is required. You have the guts. You have the juice. You have the G-A-M-E, baby. Most of you just haven't played it yet. You haven't committed, and you haven't decided. The good news is that each and every day you are granted a new gift called "time," and that equals 86,400 seconds, or 1,440 minutes.

When it comes to production and procrastination, one liberates you and one intoxicates you. The liberation from production – from a task well done, from receiving a reward, a paycheck, a payment, an override bonus, or a big check; from a task accomplished; from walking across the stage, getting an award, getting a hug from a teammate or a family member – is exhilarating to experience. On the other hand, the intoxication we derive from procrastination – the guilt, the shame, the overriding feelings of unworthiness ("I'm not good enough," "I can't believe I've done it again," "It's so big I can't possibly start") – is one of the biggest challenges with procrastination.

Procrastination Is a Left-Brain Issue

What's fascinating about procrastination is that it all happens in the left side of the brain. The left side of the brain is the egotistical mind, the mind of control. It's important to understand that procrastination is nonphysical. Its results show up physically, but it all starts out emotionally. This is where the left brain kicks in. It begins to release dopamine, and you begin to feel bad. The left brain controls your self-talk, telling you what you can't do. It starts talking about the pain that might be created. "I'll probably fail at this," "There's no way that will happen," "If I do this, this might happen," "They probably won't," "I'm not even going to go," "It will rain" – this is all the egotistical mind talking. This is the self-talk of a body that continues to stay in pain.

By contrast, a body that is experiencing pleasure releases a whole different biochemical called seratonin. This is the feel-good factor. If I could give you just one insight that will allow you to begin releasing this, it's this: Start with a simple smile – a genuine smile. This small action will create some warmth in your body, allowing you to say, "I am enough. I am lovable. I am capable." Affirmations are powerful, but they must be followed by action, because words without action are just empty statements. Affirmations without follow-through are just another set of statements that will lead to disappointment. Accomplishing your objectives begins with positive self-talk combined with affirmative action. This pattern repeated consistently and diligently over time will always lead you forward in every aspect of your life.

Beyond Motivation

What will allow you to overcome procrastination? Two situations: 1) understanding why you procrastinate and why you do what you do; and 2) creating reasons, goals, purposes, and objectives that are bigger than your procrastination issues. You develop something in your mind sight, something in your vision – something that's clear, something that motivates you.

But beyond motivation is inspiration. Inspiration is that fire in your gut. It's that passion in your core muscles, in your groin. Inspiration resides in the lower half of your body, where all your emotional, etheric energy is. It's the white-light energy called charisma that others around you can feel. They sense it, and they want to be a part of it.

Inspiration is a silent power that will carry you through your challenges. It will allow you to get back on a horse when you've been thrown off. It will allow you to get back on course when your brain's reticular activating system, otherwise known as your emotional Google search engine, has taken you off course. No matter how good you get, you will still procrastinate in isolated areas. Procrastination is an effect you can learn to address so you can eventually discover its cause.

You Are Not a Procrastinator

Here's the key to understanding how cause and effect works: You think thoughts that become feelings... feelings become moods... moods become your identity. This is the beginning of understanding that *you* are not a procrastinator. So many people say, "Oh, I'll be the first person to buy that book! I can't wait for Jeff's new *Confessions of a Recovering Procrastinator* CD to come out, because I'm such a procrastinator." Procrastination has become that individual's identity.

Instead, practice saying to yourself, "I procrastinate in isolated areas that I: 1) don't understand; 2) am learning to let go of; and 3) perceive pain." Instead of calling yourself a procrastinator, affirm that you are a recovering procrastinator. It's the twelve-step program to liberation, wealth, and joy.

The most valuable commodity you possess in this life is time. The key is turning your time into value, into service, into results, into joy, into relaxation, into production, into connection. We spend our time in two primary ways: *relaxation* and *production*. When you spend time experiencing either one of these modalities, there is so much more to gain when you are guilt-free.

Procrastination has a huge effect on both health and wealth. Have you ever put off going to the dentist or doctor? Most of us have because of the perceived anxiety of the outcome. I must admit – I procrastinate about going to the dentist. Just the thought of it is enough to keep me from making the appointment. Even though I have a really awesome dentist, it's still not enough for me to schedule a checkup.

Once I waited twelve years between dental appointments! When I finally went, I had to have a root canal and a crown; that procrastination cost me about $5,000.

Address Your Emotional Addict

The University of Windsor in Ontario reported that adult procrastinators had higher stress levels and more acute health problems than individuals who completed their tasks in a timely manner. A person is more prone to procrastinate if the task at hand seems dull, tedious, or painful. Let's face it, who gets excited about tackling a garage so full they can't get their car into it? Who wants to spend their Saturday undoing all the damage they've done to their household, dealing with all the magazines, memorabilia, and clutter they've collected over the years?

There is a tendency for the procrastinator to put off major projects until the very last minute. Remember cramming for your final exams when you were in college? I went to college in the '70s, and it wasn't uncommon for my fellow students and me to take NoDoz®, drink coffee, and use other banned substances to assist us with procrastinating.

Have you ever rushed to the airport, getting there in the nick of time to make your flight? Do you show up late to events, operating on the adrenaline rush that comes from just making the deadline? This is a common way of operating for many people. They attract attention by being late. They receive a huge jolt of adrenaline by getting in just under the wire. They wait until the pain is great enough. I know – I've experienced all of this myself.

I realized that I had a drinking problem in my twenties when I began to consume large amounts of alcohol. It was problematic enough that I started to get DUIs and had episodes of public intoxication. I knew in my creative right brain that I had a problem, but my left brain kept me in denial. My logical, egotistical mind kept me from facing it and seeking a solution. In the meantime, I kept promising myself that I would not drink, but it took me six years to achieve my first day of sobriety. Fortunately for me, since that very first day, I've never had another drink. This is an example of allowing procrastination to reach a problematic stage, to the point that I almost had to die to change. This is not the ideal way to address an emotional addiction.

Risk and Reward

The amount of time before a project due date also impacts the probability of procrastination. We are more likely to put off a task when the deadline is far away. This happens because of the phenomena known as "temporal delay," which means that the further a person is from a reward or a feeling of accomplishment, and the less certain that person feels about reaching the end result, he or she is more likely to resist performing the required action necessary to earn it. Another way of saying this is that immediate gratification is more motivating than prizes or accolades received as a reward for tasks accomplished in the future. The risk or reward factor is much greater when the reward is closer, right there in front of you.

The characteristic most commonly linked to procrastination is a lack of conscientiousness. A person who is highly conscientious and organized is usually industrious and productive. This describes me. I'm very organized. I'm very productive.

I have a method; I have a routine. But not everyone in my family is as perfectionistic or organized as I am. Individuals who are not conscientious have a high probability of procrastinating.

If you have a lot of chaos and a lot of drama in your life, the first step you want to take is to forgive yourself. Don't judge yourself. If you have a mountain of clutter to tackle, don't look at it and hyperventilate. When you react this way, your body goes into fight-or-flight mode.

Highly impulsive people are also prone to procrastinate. Temptation is an easy way to lead the procrastinator off course. Procrastinators are constantly behind their own eight ball, waiting until the last minute to run in and rescue themselves. They live for the adrenaline rush followed by a major letdown. They are addicted emotionally and chemically to experiencing high highs and low lows. Brain chemistry – adrenaline, coritsol, dopamine, serotonin, and emotional mind/body connection – can explain this. The brain gets addicted to both the chemicals released in our bodies during highly emotional states, as well as the chemicals released immediately once these events have transpired.

Procrastination and Anxiety

Procrastination is also directly linked to anxiety, which is an offshoot of neuroticism. Getting started is easily postponed because of the anxiety of failure. The subconscious internal dialogue sounds something like, "I'm afraid I won't do it perfectly; I'll make a mistake. I'll lose the prospect or friend. I won't be able to live up to my standards. I'm not prepared enough." There are many other reasons, justifications, validations, and just flat-out excuses.

And the definition of an excuse is just a well-planned lie.

The words (and sometimes even the sounds) we use create our procrastination. Have you ever asked someone a question and the first sound of his or her mouth was "Um," followed by the preposition "Well..."? In this situation, the person is actually procrastinating before articulating. When you ask them a question, they immediately check out and go into their left brain. Instead of saying what they feel, they go into thinking mode; instead of feeling, they're logical. When they finally start talking, they usually begin to justify and validate themselves rather than speak from their true intuition.

Neurotic Perfectionism

There are two forms of perfection: *practical perfection* and *neurotic perfection*. You can be neurotic in your own perfection. You can be an absolutely organized, detailed, neurotic perfectionist. We'll be exploring this type of procrastinator in much more detail in Chapter Two, but for now, suffice it to say, if your desire for perfection keeps you from production, then there's a high probability that it's a neurosis.

If you can turn your neurotic perfection into a practical perfection that rewards you (a task well done, feeling good about a situation, meticulous in certain areas), then it's healthy. But if you're so neurotic that you can't start, if you're so neurotic you can't leave (and you've probably heard of people who have fear of flying, or fear of driving in a car, or fear of leaving their house), these are phobias that are also symptoms of procrastination.

Individuals caught inside one of these phobias don't feel in control of a particular situation, but what they *can* control is staying home. If they don't fly, they won't get killed in an airline accident. If they don't get on a train, they won't be involved in a train wreck. If they don't drive, they won't get into a car wreck. Instead of experiencing these forms of transportation, they practice procrastination. They can control the outcome by staying home, but then they say, "I can't take a trip," "Oh, I wished I would have," or "I've got to find a pill to "cure" my condition – blue pill, red pill, etc."

Remember the line from that Huey Lewis and the News song, "I want a new drug, one that don't make me nervous"? That's what happens to a lot of us. We are conditioned to take any number of over-the-counter or prescription medications to address our anxieties and mask our feelings. Some of us are told that we're too creative. We have ADD. We have anxiety. We have sleep disorders. We are given a series of pills to address our feelings, and we end up dumbing down our creativity.

Addressing the Reasons Why

To really let go, it is your responsibility to understand why you do what you do. Did you grow up with procrastinators? Did you grow up with neurotic perfectionists? Did you grow up with a practical perfectionist? Were you always told what you had to do? Were you reprimanded if you didn't do what you were told? Did you rebel against order? When you went to college or moved out of your house, did you stop making your bed out of rebellion?

These are some of the areas you must address. If you don't, you'll just continue to put off the situation until the last minute, validating that if it is done poorly, the expectations won't have to be so high the next time, thus reducing the pressure to succeed.

Two key elements play a large part in the urge to postpone projects: Uncertain feelings about an activity and the desire to avoid discomfort. The procrastinator's self-talk says, "I'm not sure if the timing is right," thus avoiding the risk of failure. Indecision also plays a large role in the conscious/unconscious mind of the procrastinator. This person cannot make up their mind. Actually, they *can* make up their mind, but they tell themselves that they can't. They choose not to decide. It's not that they can't; it's just that they don't.

They decide that they require more training, a new website, a weekend seminar, a life coach, a mentor, someone to model themselves after. All of these things can be liberating if they are applied practically. But merely going through the step-by-step process and never applying the knowledge just produces a seminar junkie who continues to procrastinate.

Nothing is ever perfect enough for a large percent of the procrastinators in the world, allowing them to justify their constant lack of commitment. Many procrastinators believe they require the pressure of a last minute deadline to justify the dragging of their feet, which they then justify to avoid the pain of what they perceive they may lose as a result of their decision. They justify themselves by saying, "If I would've started earlier, then I would have executed perfectly." This justification masks low self-esteem that is a key component to their performance anxiety, which in turn causes the procrastination in the first place.

24

Breaking the Procrastinator Identity

Most procrastinators would love to break their procrastinator identity, but it has become so engrained in them that it is automatic. In order to break this identity, begin right now by saying, "I procrastinate in isolated areas that I perceive pain or rebel against. I am not a procrastinator. I have started the process of becoming a recovering procrastinator."

If you say to yourself, "Oh, this always happens," then it becomes a certainty. A certainty is a belief, which then becomes an expectation. If you allow your expectations to define you, they will either liberate you or intoxicate you. Case in point: If you are very good at attracting money, and you expect to attract money, there's a high probability that you *will* attract money, especially if you have had success in doing that. And if you have become a money magnet, there's a high probability that people will show up to reinforce your feelings.

You attract to your reality situations and people that fulfill a biochemical craving you are addicted to. Telepathically and emotionally, you send a set of signals based on what you're thinking and/or feeling. If the feelings you are sending come from a self-esteem that's very low – you have been abandoned and neglected, you've been abused, you've been traumatized – you will attract the perpetrators and other types of people that you don't want to show up. You will attract the kind of people who will bring conflict rather than collaboration.

Even though you would love to break your feelings of procrastination, doing this requires a whole new philosophy. If you just try to be positive, all you're really doing is taking a spray can of motivation and coating your procrastinator rust. To *really* change, you require transformation. On an emotional level, you learn to transform those feelings that create the very situation that hinders you. When procrastination becomes chronic, you are essentially running on autosuggestion. To break the procrastination habit, you begin by addressing the causes, not the effects.

Raising Your Consciousness Level

What events began your procrastination habit? Over time, the more you understand why you do what you do, the more awareness you develop. The word "awareness" is synonymous with consciousness. Raising your level of awareness raises your level of consciousness, your level of energy, and the level of how you feel about yourself. What you require is love – self-love – and no one will give it to you because it is permission based. And the only person who can give you permission is you.

What you require is self-esteem, not self-confidence. Confidence is how you feel about *something*. Self-esteem is how you feel about *yourself*. The real question is, "What do you do while you're living? Who are you? And what are you becoming?" You want to be able to live your life as a vocation.

For most people, the ultimate desire is owning a life that does not own them. Your most valuable commodity is time, but if procrastination is the thief of your time, then what you have is a developing situation. And that developing situation will create another situation – NFL: no friends left, no funds left, and not for long. That is what happens to a large percentage of the population. They have an intention, but an intention is not the same as a commitment or a decision. Once someone follows through on a true commitment, they can create any result they truly desire. But the downfall for many individuals is that they just take on more businesses, more obligations, and more situations. They get overwhelmed, and they procrastinate.

Let's Get Realistic

The solution is to create clearly defined goals, not overwhelming, overstated goals that cause you to procrastinate before you even start. I asked one of my clients recently, "How much income do you desire to achieve from the comfort of your home during this calendar year?"

He replied, "Well, let's shoot for $200,000."

I said, "Let's not."

I continued, "Let's get realistic. Do you have a $200,000-a-year habit?"

"Do I have a $200,000-a-year habit?"

"You are repeating my question."

"What was your question?"

This is a perfect example of someone who is "lost in his sauce." He's someone I really care about, but he created a goal that was so big that he couldn't possibly begin to achieve it.

He had no idea what I meant when I said, "Do you have a $200,000-a-year habit?"

In 2008, psychologist Shane Owens and his colleagues at Hofstra University demonstrated that procrastinators who perform implementation commitments were nearly eight times more likely to follow through on a commitment than those who did not create them. When you become clear and concise in your words and your language, you will begin to exude a sense of silent power. This is known as emotional, etheric energy or charisma. Others sense when this type of energy permeates you. It's your juice, your drive. It's the inspiration that will carry you through obstacles, challenges, and entrepreneurial seizure.

Just Do It

My advice to procrastinators is to follow Nike's simple, effective advice: "Just do it." The word procrastination comes from the Latin verb *procrastinare*, meaning "to put off until tomorrow." For the procrastinator, avoidance becomes a way of life. To be productive in life requires understanding and releasing procrastination. Survival often depends on completing simple tasks, such as planting and harvesting crops in a timely and effective manner. This is the difference between survival and flourishing, between just getting by and being extremely prosperous.

Procrastination is reflected in the folklore and proverbs of many cultures. You are probably familiar with a few of the following sayings that reflect our feelings about procrastination:

"Don't put off until tomorrow what you can do today."

"A stitch in time saves nine."

"One of these days is none of these days." (English saying)

"Between saying and doing, many a pair of shoes is worn out." (Italian saying)

"Procrastination is the thief of time." (Edward Young, 1742)

Procrastination is more than a time-management issue. As many of you have discovered when you've attempted to reduce procrastination, improved time-management techniques typically prove ineffective. Why? Because you can't manage time. Time is much more about managing yourself daily than arbitrarily managing a clock.

Procrastination, Indecision, and Disappointment

Procrastination is not the same as indecision. While indecision implies the inability to decide, procrastination occurs when a person creates a decision but does not follow through with it. It is possible to procrastinate during the decision-making process. However, this type of procrastination is not seen as inherently different from other postponed tasks. Procrastination is a complex behavior composed of logical, emotional, and behavioral components. Procrastination is the tendency to postpone or avoid reaching a described goal, with the subconscious intention of remaining disappointed. Of course, that's also the definition of insanity: doing the same thing over and over, expecting a different result.

It's a hard pill to swallow when you realize that you're addicted to disappointment. You have good intentions, but you have no decision, no commitment, and so you end up disappointed. Think about how much of today's society is addicted to disappointment.

Goals are personal, and they are a lot are like beauty – they are held in the eye of the beholder. What seems like a worthy goal to you might not have the same priority for someone else. However, when a task has value to you, but your behavior does not follow through with action to complete the task, procrastination is occurring.

Procrastination also occurs when small steps are not taken to achieve important, long-term goals. This illustrates again why so many people set lofty, colossal goals that are not achievable, thus creating an excuse to procrastinate, feel bad, and remain disappointed. In the book *Overcoming Procrastination,* psychologists Albert Ellis and William Knaus define procrastination as "delaying task completion to the point of experiencing discomfort."

Overcoming Procrastination One Day at a Time

Procrastination is a tendency to avoid commitment, decision creation, discomfort, pain, failure, and, most of all, success. Deadlines get missed. Late fees build up. Commitments are avoided. Family and friends get upset. Disappointment and resentment builds. Guilt and shame mount, and what were once good intentions become a source of disappointment. Does this sound familiar?

Procrastination occurs when there is no real passion to action. It is difficult to assess why any of us procrastinate because of the self-defeating nature of the outcome. It is irrational not to desire change in the areas of our lives that do not serve us.

A lack of planning is common among those who are habitual procrastinators. Those who live with very little structure tend to end up overwhelmed with all their delayed projects and goals. The rebellious personality is proud of nonconformity to the extreme, so much so that they rebel against their own success. Rebelling to the point of having no plan is, in fact, planning to fail.

Procrastination is perpetuated by good intentions combined with bad habits. Overcoming procrastination is like addressing any addiction; it is accomplished one day at a time. You commit to change one day at a time, to let go one day at a time. You teach yourself to let go of feelings, events, people, violations, abandonment, situations, and rejection. It can take one day, one block of time, one hour – whatever is required for you to release the feelings that create the cause.

Remember, it's the cause that creates the effect. When you begin to address the cause, letting go of procrastination opens up a whole new awareness for you. It's whatever causes procrastination in the first place that keeps you doing the same thing over and over, always expecting a different result. Overcoming procrastination becomes easier when the cause is identified and new systems are implemented to begin changing one day at a time. The action must follow the plan, or all you have accomplished is establishing another situation for procrastination.

Routine daily tasks may not seem like goals, yet simple situations like finishing the laundry, taking out the trash, getting the groceries, walking the dogs, and exercising are actually subgoals within the main goal of maintaining a level of daily order. And be assured, that daily order will definitely show up in your career or your enterprise.

Life imitates business, and business imitates life. If you have bad habits in your life, those habits, unfortunately, will follow you into all of your other endeavors. But don't despair. Every single one of us has the ability to transform rapidly. The Latin definition of prosperity is "in the flow." Procrastination occurs when small steps towards larger goals are avoided. Procrastination is neutralized when small steps are consistently implemented with a greater purpose in mind and a clear, manageable, attainable goal as the desired outcome.

Procrastination is a learned behavior, but certain hardwired personality traits increase the likelihood that a person will assume this behavior. Procrastination is the dance between the brain and the situation. In the next chapters, we'll look at the profiles of six types of procrastinators and discover strategies for overcoming procrastination, no matter who you are.

NOTES

NOTES

2
THE NEUROTIC PERFECTIONIST

The first type of procrastinator is the **neurotic perfectionist.** The neurotic perfectionist is a very unique type of procrastinator, and I myself have been in this very situation a time... or two hundred. I tend to be critical. I tend to be all-or-nothing. I tend to put a lot of judgment on myself and end up judging others. This all leads to control.

Just to be clear, I have just as many flaws as the next person. Over the last twenty-five years, however, I've taken a deep look at why I do what I do. My motivation now is to assist you, as well as assist myself, to understand these two very key words when it comes to transformation – *letting go.*

Characteristics of the Neurotic Perfectionist

The neurotic perfectionist is very critical and very judgmental of other people – but they are especially critical of themselves. This person can't start something until it's actually absolutely perfect. Neurotic perfectionists tend to have an all-or-nothing type of personality.

The neurotic perfectionist wants to be flawless – so flawless that they become paralyzed. This person is usually extremely meticulous in their style and mannerisms. They're very neat; they're very controlled. They tend to wear dark colors – dark gray, black, navy. They often wear glasses. They are very intelligent; this is the most intelligent sector of society. Their desire to be flawless makes them very anxious.

Of all the procrastinator types, they usually have the most anxiety, and they are the most prone to depression.

Neurotic perfectionists have a psychological desire for control, but this doesn't mean that they want to control others. Instead, they want to be in control in their left brain. This is why procrastination becomes so prevalent for them – they're so neurotic that they can't stomach the thought of failing, and so they stay perfect. They become neurotic in their perfection by controlling everything between their two ears. In this way, they don't fail, but they do end up disappointed.

A neurotic perfectionist takes perfection to such a degree that they don't have time for anyone else. This personality can't possibly have true relationships because the only relationships they experience are the ones that disappoint them. Neurotic perfectionists often end up in divorce because they're so compulsive that no one can connect with them. I know – I've been there.

I used to intellectualize people out of my life because they weren't perfect enough for me. Because of this, I waited a long time to get married. When I finally did marry, I had challenges; I had been a bachelor for so long that no one could ever fit into my box. Eventually I learned that if I was ever going to have peace or love, I had to adapt, change, and let go of control.

It's funny to look back on now, but it wasn't then – dirt, hair, all kinds of things used to drive me crazy. Everything had to be perfect. I would vacuum in rows. I had a vacuum cleaner in every room in my house. I know it sounds ridiculous, but for me it was a level of control. As I learned to let go of some of this neurotic perfection, I discovered some amazing people in my life.

They were always there, but I wasn't emotionally available to let them in. As I started to let go, the people that were always there started to reward me. I began to experience collaboration instead of competition.

Experiencing this is very liberating. Rather than being intoxicated in your neurotic perfection, suddenly the people that have always been waiting to show up are there. I'll never forget one of the biggest years I ever had in my career financially. People said, "What happened to you?" I just smiled and said to myself, "Well, I let go." Only someone who had been through the same situation would have understood this. I hope that, as you read this, you will get my message that in order to achieve success you absolutely require collaboration with other people in your life.

Neurotic perfectionists prefer to work alone. That's why they tend to gravitate to careers where they are isolated. A lot neurotic perfectionists work in the computer industry, or they become architects or scientists. They are the classic doers, but they tend to overwork and yet not get a lot done. They get intoxicated with how much they're accomplishing, but in reality, they don't accomplish very much because it takes them so long to complete a task.

Neurotic perfectionists become so absorbed in what they're doing that they don't accomplish much in the end. They develop an addiction to busyness. However, all this busyness does not usually result in profit. As business owners, neurotic perfectionists usually have huge challenges. In a controlled environment, where they're employees, an employer can sometimes get a lot out of them. However, when they are on their own, they tend to obsess.

The neurotic perfectionist has trouble setting reasonable, realistic time limits to complete projects. They typically don't operate well on deadlines because they obsess about having everything perfect. They write and rewrite. They go through revision after revision. They can't turn it in. They can't start because it has to be absolutely perfect. They have to have the right script. They have to have the right story. They have to have the right details. They have to create the right situation. It has to be the perfect setting. They have to join the right company, and consequently they will jump from company to company, situation to situation. It's absolutely exhausting.

Neurotic perfectionists wait until the last minute to complete things. They get a great deal of adrenaline from this. They rush in to rescue themselves. They wait to the last minute to do their taxes. They wait to the last minute to write their content for their blogs. They wait until the deadline is upon them to finish a project. They wait to the last minute to leave for the airport. This becomes a huge part of their personality, and they are always late for everything.

This might stem from being the youngest child in a family, or being an only child that was neglected and forgotten. When they waited until the last minute, people noticed them. In their minds, bad love is better than no love.

For instance, one of my clients confided to me that he was the last child of eight, with several years between him and his siblings. By the time that he was born, his mother and father were just worn out. He learned that the way to get attention was being late for everything. He was late for church; he was late for school. He was always getting reprimanded, even though he was highly capable. As an adult, he was late getting to the airport, late for work, late for appointments.

While he always seemed to get a great deal of attention, this didn't serve him later in life because he tended to get fired.

Neurotic perfectionists set unrealistic goals and then become paralyzed by them. If this description fits you, it's time to become objective. There's a huge amount of pressure on entrepreneurs, self-employed salespeople, and those in direct sales to set goals. We are taught to write our goals down. Have big, hairy, audacious goals. Have goals bigger than our problems. And, of course, there *is* merit to that. However, if you set goals that are so big they paralyze you, it's not conducive to your progress.

The neurotic perfectionist relies on skills and talent alone. This personality type tends to have a big ego and a smaller bank account. This is a generalization, of course, but as a general rule, this type of person is so smart that they rely on intelligence and talent, and they don't typically manifest the habits required to become successful.

The neurotic perfectionist vacillates between giving everything and giving nothing. Being all-or-nothing gives them a big rush. They rush to the airport, and they give it everything they have just to make that gate. And they cross that line, that finish line, and they get in that seat, but they don't get there on time. Success is not like that; success is a methodical process. Success is much more of a *relaxed* intensity rather than an *intense* intensity. Intense intensity creates adrenaline, and neurotic perfectionists can virtually get addicted to that adrenaline.

This is where the term "adrenaline junkie" comes from. These are people who love to skydive, bungee-jump, and engage in all sorts of other daredevil-type activities. They like to ski off cliffs.

But that kind of attitude in business doesn't lead to success. We've all seen football players bang their heads against each other or do inverted back flips. This fuels their adrenaline, and they go out and win a championship. But they can't live like that, and that's why so many athletes and performers have challenges when their career is over. Neurotic perfectionists try to control control and instead end up out of control. Being overwhelmed keeps them from breaking through. This personality type wakes up overwhelmed and goes to bed overwhelmed. They get overwhelmed by all the energy they have. Eventually, in this state of overwhelm, they shut down.

The neurotic perfectionist consistently turns potential allies into adversaries. They often alienate the very people they desire to have in their life because of their insistence on being right. They like to argue. They like to be right. A lot of times, great people show up in their life, but they end up alienating them because they like to be in conflict.

This was a huge part of my struggle. I was very good at sales and closing. During the first several years of my business career, I would look at my sales organization and discover that no one was producing. I attracted the kind of individuals that I could take care of, that I could rescue, that I could do everything for. Unfortunately, I alienated the kind of people I really required in my life; I would create conflict, and then I would end up resenting them because they didn't see things my way.

Neurotic perfectionists strive for perfection rather than excellence. Neurotic perfectionists are human doings. They are machines. They're mechanical; they're not emotional. This is usually because they tried to live up to the expectations of someone in their circle of influence. It's not always a parent – it might be a clergyman, a coach, an older sibling, or a teacher. Maybe they brought home an A, and it wasn't an A+. They scored twenty points in a basketball game, but it wasn't thirty. If something wasn't perfect, then it wasn't enough. As this pattern developed, they began to believe, "I am not enough." If this strikes a chord with you, begin to affirm: "I am enough."

Neurotic perfectionists fear failure, and it becomes the reason to put off getting started. They are seldom ever satisfied. Once again, they strive for perfection rather than excellence. Perfection is disappointment before it starts because there is no perfection unless your perfection is relaxed. Remember, 100 percent perfection is impossible.

Someone is going to cross your path. Someone is going to say something that affects you. An affirmation that I've been using for several years goes like this: "I never have a bad day, only a few challenging moments." If you can begin to live in that modality, you will have productive days.

The neurotic perfectionist procrastinates because they just might not be able to live up to their own expectations. Neurotic perfectionists get seduced by how brilliant they are, how intelligent they are, how smart they are, how good they look... and they *do* look good. They have a lot of entitlement issues because of their intelligence, their skills, and their talent. Did you ever score so high in a class that you got noticed? Did you ever do so well that you got ostracized? Were you better than other people in your class in school, or in certain situations that you got moved ahead, and then the pressure became so great that you collapsed?

I once coached a client whose son was on David Letterman as a saxophonist when he was nine years old. I saw the woman several years later, and I asked her whatever happened to her son. He went into software engineering. He was a virtuoso saxophone player, but he was so burned out on music by the time he was eighteen that he just wanted to go to college and fit in.

Often, even though neurotic perfectionists look good, they feel bad, and they cover that up with ego. An ego doesn't necessarily mean being arrogant, rude, or abrasive. It's typically a mask that keeps other people at a distance. An ego is a way to stay hidden behind your false self and not really let people feel, sense, or be a part of you. An ego is how you live in your pain. An ego is how you live in your past. It is incredibly liberating to let go of your ego.

The word "ego" doesn't mean what you typically think it means. Eckhart Tolle said it so well in his brilliant book, *The Power of Now.* He calls it the "pain body." The ego is really the unconscious, where you stay in pain. You don't feel comfortable risking pleasure, so you procrastinate; you end up disappointed, yet you never fail.

The neurotic perfectionist has challenges meeting deadlines. They overcomplicate situations. They fall behind, and then they have to rush in to rescue themselves. I call this the "Sir Galahad complex." One of their main excuses is that they don't allow enough time. However, they end up killing time because of their procrastination.

I once assisted a client to write content for an award he was going to receive. I gave him the outline for the content, and he worked on it, and worked on it, and worked on it. He kept calling me – to the point that it became exhausting. He would ask me the same question over and over. I would say, "I already did that for you. I did that for you a week ago, two weeks ago, three weeks ago, a month ago, two months ago."

I didn't hear from him for a while, and when I did, I asked him how he did on his speech. He said, "Oh, I blew it – I didn't have enough time to complete it." I just shook my head; he had two months to do it, but he waited until the very last minute. He kept rewriting it, starting completely over. Finally, he slapped something together at the last minute.

Keys to Releasing the Neurotic Perfectionist

Now, let's take a look at how to release and let go of all of this. First of all, take a look in your rearview mirror and ask some yourself some quality questions. "If I'm a neurotic perfectionist, that's an effect. What is my cause? When did this become my identity? How did I get trapped in this situation? What am I willing to do to let go?"

You may not have the answers right now, but as you begin to understand why you do what you do, you'll develop an entirely different level of awareness. When you have one of these "aha" moments, it's God winking. That's synchronicity… synchrodestiny… a breakthrough… a quantum leap. Transformation is the real power that allows you to let go. This requires changing how you've been feeling, changing how you've been changing.

If you continue to do what you do, then you will continue to operate in that which is familiar. To let go of this requires inspiration. You must become serious about letting go. You must have reasons that are bigger than your problems. If your problems are bigger than your reasons, there's a high probability you'll continue to tiptoe quietly through life, arriving safely at your grave. You will have lived the greatest pain you can possibly live, the pain of regret. Drive by any garden of stones (that would be a cemetery) – it is filled with people who had potential – unrealized potential.

You have potential. You are in the right place at the right time, but you must recognize it. This requires energy and synergy, feelings and emotions. You have to be willing to trade risk for reward. You have to step into the big league. You have to throw the pass. You have to run the race. You have to risk not being perfect.

People don't care if you're perfect; they care if you get results. They care if you care. They care if you're human. People aren't looking for robots and machines; they're looking for emotional beings. They want to see your rawness, not your perfect state. They want to see your hair messed up. They want to see you with your mascara running down your face. Believe it or not, people love to see you cry. Not the cry of regret, not the cry of being a victim, but the real tears that roll down your face when you're having a breakthrough; tears of joy; tears of compassion. This kind of transparency inspires people.

Being the Best Is Overrated

If you want to release your identity as a neurotic perfectionist, I'm not suggesting that you let go of perfection. I myself am a perfectionist; I grew up that way. There are many areas of perfection that serve me. However, I have learned that *good is enough*. Being the best is overrated.

It's a state you can never reach because there's always someone better, someone better looking, someone more talented, or someone more intelligent.

You don't have to be the best. How about being *your* best? And your best does not have to be 100 percent. Rather than being a neurotic perfectionist, how about being a *practical perfectionist*? Not only do you want to be a *practical* perfectionist, you want to be a *productive* perfectionist.

Change Your Philosophy to Achieve Practical Results

I lived many years of my life as a neurotic perfectionist, hiding behind alcohol and drugs. My self-esteem that was so low that my vibration didn't even register on the Richter scale. I attempted to take my life when I was twenty-eight years old because I had so much pain – even though I also had so much talent. People would tell me how good I was, and I just didn't see it. It took me getting clean and sober at age thirty-two, and then it took me another eight years before I had one of my biggest breakthroughs.

You don't have to wait years and years. Isn't it time to let go right now? Not tomorrow, not next week, not next year – and you can't do it yesterday. What's amazing about the human body is that it regenerates cells. You can change your DNA as you change the way you feel. You can change your whole physique just by a few simple disciplines implemented over a period of time.

If you're a neurotic perfectionist, right now you can begin to affirm that you are a "practical perfectionist." When I was forty years old, I heard the phrase "relaxed intensity" instead of "intensity." Those two words changed my life. For the first time in my life, I realized that I didn't have to grind the enamel down on the left side of my teeth, creating TMJ. Words like "peace" were foreign to me – the only peace I ever heard in my entire vocabulary was "peace treaty." I thought that surrendering was a sign of weakness.

When I first heard the word "surrender" used in personal development circles, I thought only weak people surrendered or countries that lost in battle. When I learned that surrender really means surrendering my will and surrendering my ego, surrendering my desire to be right and having to be so perfect that no one could connect with me, I started to change the way I look at situations. And you can do the same!

If you are so perfect that you have no one in your life, I have a news flash for you. Perhaps what you're doing isn't getting rewards. If you have "pennies in your pocket, zero in your bank account, and the creditors calling," as the great Jim Rohn used to say, then perhaps it's time to change your philosophy. If neurotic perfection is just leading you to procrastination, isn't it time for you to utilize procrastination and neurotic perfection to attain practical results?

Methodically Letting Go

If you see yourself in these pages, what is the next step? First, recognize that you didn't get this way overnight. If you have a lot of clutter, a lot of chaos, a lot of drama, and most importantly, a lot of stuff, it's not going to go away overnight. Create a systematic, detailed, methodical approach to relieving yourself of this situation. If nothing else, call someone to come in and assist you. If that's not in the financial cards, you can do it yourself. Start with one corner. Get yourself two thirty-three-gallon bags. Throw away everything you are willing to let go of in a fifteen-minute time frame. It's very liberating, believe me. I have assisted many, many clients to do this. Continue to do a little bit more over an extended period of time.

It's similar to writing a book. When I wrote one of my previous books, I started by writing two pages a night for twenty consecutive nights. *Voilà*, after twenty nights I had forty pages! After 100 nights in a row, I had a 200-page book. Success is achieved over a period of time. Once again, it's not so much about what you do, it's what you do daily.

Objectivity Is the Objective

There's a lot of content in this chapter because the neurotic perfectionist has a lot of energy. They have a lot of excitement, a lot of adrenaline, a lot of juice – but they must learn how to contain it. The goal is to have *low highs* and *high lows*, not *high highs* and *low lows*.

For the neurotic perfectionist, getting started is key. If this is your personality, ask yourself, "What did I accomplish today?" Write out just a few, simple tasks that you desire to accomplish tomorrow. Don't have twenty-five tasks to accomplish in a day. That becomes the perfect excuse not to start.

You might also find yourself doing too much for other people, setting those individuals up to disappoint you so that you can then resent them. Very few people will perform to a neurotic perfectionist's capabilities and standards. As you begin to understand that, you won't put so much pressure on yourself and others.

Being a neurotic perfectionist means living with a lot of guilt and shame, and there are often underlying issues from past events that create this behavior. When you learn to let go of your past, you'll no longer be stuck in it, and you can live fully in the present. The more you live in the present, the more you'll live in a more relaxed type of perfection.

Becoming Practically Excellent

It's time to be realistic. Let go of any entitlement issues. Just because you've been successful in one area doesn't mean you're entitled to be successful in a new vocation, a new modality, a new way of living, a new way of healing. Success requires practicality, objectivity, and most of all, the courage to be you.

You can't be a superstar overnight. This requires patience. Progress is only created by what you do daily. One thing is for sure – you won't get there by procrastinating. You'll get there by producing. Instead of being a neurotic perfectionist that accomplishes nothing, your goal is to become a practical perfectionist that produces results.

Let go of the word "perfection" and substitute the word "excellence" instead. You can also explore using the words "good," "great," "realistic," or "objective." These words allow you to release the pressure you put on yourself from your logical, practical, egoistical mind. Success is about being realistic. Success is methodical. Success is a system. Success is a science.

Take what you've received from this chapter and find a way to apply it practically. The neurotic perfectionist has a tendency to read material over and over, taking notes and writing everything down. Taking notes is overrated, and applying practical knowledge is underrated. This insight will unequivocally allow you to transform the way you feel about yourself, so that you can become a much more practical perfectionist.

NOTES

NOTES

3
THE BIG DEAL CHASER

Procrastinator type number two is **the big deal chaser** – the "big hat/no cattle syndrome." This is one of the most interesting identities of all six procrastinator types, and one of the most seductive. Big deal chasers have great energy. They're very witty. They're intelligent. They're suave. They look good, but underneath their good looks they really feel bad. Big deal chasers are the biggest dreamers of the six procrastinator types.

Characteristics of the Big Deal Chaser

Big deal chasers have lots of energy and good people skills. But those positive qualities have to be applied to the kind of enterprise that will reward them. Big hat/no cattle procrastinators usually have good intentions, poor habits, and above-average skills. They tend to mask their low self-esteem with high confidence. Being articulate promoters, they are often able to persuade others to buy into their idealistic dreams. However, the dreams they dream are so big that the idea of achieving them creates paralysis and procrastination. Their capacity to dream turns into a liability rather than an asset.

Big deal chasers are idealistic. They live in their vision and their dreams, but they have challenges developing the habits and skills required to actualize either. In other words, they have entitlement issues. They embrace huge causes. They have big real estate projects. They're going to change the world. When it comes to their emotional style, they're often very vague. They have big dreams, but they usually don't have a plan or a system that matches those dreams. Big deal chasers think that fate will intervene and eliminate the required effort for them to become successful. They feel blessed, special, unique, chosen, and angelic.

They're intoxicated with their own greatness, and they live in delusion and denial. They live on wishes. I use to sit around and say, "If I had three wishes, one of those wishes would be a thousand wishes so I'd never run out of wishes."

Big deal chasers are passive. Even though they're idealistic, they often are very passive about their dreams. They sound passionate, but just underneath all those big dreams is a low self-esteem – they really don't believe they deserve success. But dreams are intoxicating, and so they move from project to project. Their talk is big, but their results are few, and those that know them have witnessed a pattern of projects started, then abandoned before completion. The big deal chaser often is very charismatic and has a team of devoted followers who pick up the pieces and neutralize the damage after they have moved on to the next "big thing."

Big deal chasers have lots of excuses. They are not detail-oriented. They are very unrealistic about what is required to develop daily habits, or perform daily disciplines. In their minds, they don't have to master the ordinary skills that successful people – normal business owners and entrepreneurs – master. They avoid problems, hardships, and responsibilities that are necessary to become successful, prosperous, and fulfilled.

Big deal chasers have entitlement issues. They typically think that they are better than the rest of society. Not better human beings, but superior ideas. They don't have to do what everyone else does. They drift from career to career, waiting for that mythical moment when someone will recognize their brilliance. Magically, the world's talent scouts will spot their talent, their potential. They dream of making it big as speakers or authors. They're going to write a hit song. They're going to be discovered.

Big deal chasers have a "Sir Galahad complex." They take on big projects and big causes. This is very seductive. There's always someone who will magically ride into town and rescue them. One of their ideas is going to be the one that bales them out. When they hit rock bottom, they typically hit rock bottom the hardest. Big-deal chasers suffer a great deal of frustration and self-doubt because of the space between their big deal dreams and what is really required to achieve those dreams. They want their dreams without the effort, and they quit easily when difficulty, challenges, and adversity arise.

Does this sound like you? Perhaps you have a family member that's a big deal chaser, someone who always has a scheme – some situation that's so big, it's going to rescue the whole family. This happened to me back in the mid-1990s – I got seduced into an investment situation that I believed would rescue me from the credit card debt I had acquired through a failed business venture. Instead of rescuing me, I ended up over $100,000 in debt. I went from one failed business venture to another, seeking to be rescued instead of methodically making the good, old-fashioned effort required over a long period of time. I spent an entire year chasing that big deal; eventually the bottom fell out, and I was left with over $100,000 of liability.

Big deal chasers are prone to addiction. This personality type is very addictive. This is why people get intoxicated with the lottery, romancing about what they're going do when they hit that jackpot. Of course, *someone* wins the lottery, so I'm not saying that you shouldn't play. But you can't base your circumstances around the fact that you're going to be that one in a trillion who wins the big money.

Big deal chasers tend to be great talkers. Words like "hip," "slick," and "cool" apply to this type of personality type.

One of the most interesting people I've ever coached was someone who fooled even me. This gentleman was very handsome. He was a military professional who had graduated from one of the renowned academies. He then went on to have a very distinguished service career, or so he said. As an entrepreneur, he was a great presenter, a real showman. He could motivate an audience, keeping them on the edge of their seats. But a year or so after I met him, I started to see a crack in his veneer. I noticed that he had a lot of financial challenges. I found out later that he had borrowed lots of money. You guessed it – he was a big deal chaser. Big deal chasers can leave a lot of people in their wake. They don't mean to hurt people. They don't mean to burn people. If they borrow money from people, they definitely intend to pay it back. They carry a lot of debt, and they often create a lot of debt for their family and friends.

If You Created It, You Can Uncreate It!

Maybe you recognize yourself in the above descriptions. Perhaps you're in the process of recovering from a big deal, and you have lots of debt left over from this situation. Either way, take a deep breath before you go on reading. *No matter what you created, you can uncreate it.*

I'm not talking about taking the easy way out. The easy way out would be to walk away from your problems, file bankruptcy, or walk away from your home, go through foreclosure. I'm talking about developing the character and the courage to really engage in a recovery process.

What if you're married to a big-deal chaser? Don't despair, because often these people are some of the top producers in the world. Every single one of us can change.

Isn't it time to let go? Isn't it time to change? You can't procrastinate forever. You can't get ready to get ready forever. This isn't about perfection. It's not about knowing all the details. It's about practicing the art of simple discipline, so that some of the details start to manifest into a compounded effect. You don't develop wealth habits by big deal chasing. You develop wealth habits by getting money right. Fame is overrated. Success is how you feel about yourself.

Don't Just Set the Goal – Get the Goal

Of course it's important to dream big and set goals. But if you *set* a goal, it's equally important to *get* the goal. There isn't anyone reading this book that can't climb Mount Everest or write a hit song. You could potentially write a best seller. But you'll never write a best seller unless you start writing those first two pages.

Do you realize that simple, methodical disciplines engaged in over a long period of time are what will allow you to write your first book? If you just wrote two pages a day for a hundred consecutive days, you'd have your first book. Now, if you read those words and automatically thought to yourself, *Well, that sounds easy, but I don't like to write,* I can appreciate that. I said that for years, and then I realized that for me to ever finish writing a book, I'd have to practice a different level of discipline.

We all procrastinate in isolated areas where we feel anxiety. Are you ready to address your procrastination issues? Are you realistically ready to let go of the feelings that create your procrastination identity? Are you willing to take a look at the cause that creates the effect? If you are, that's a victory. For instance, if you carry excess weight, it's not just dieting and exercise that will allow you to live in the physique that you deserve.

It's being able to let go of the feelings that keep you doing the same thing over and over, expecting different results.

Rebuild Your Bridges

In the traditional twelve-step program, one step is to take a fearless, moral inventory of yourself and how you approach others, and then ask for forgiveness. I put that my own words, but that's the essence of it. If you are a big deal chaser, take a moral inventory of yourself. Ask yourself if there are people you've hurt or bridges you've burned. If it's possible, go back to those people and ask them to forgive you. If you've created unfavorable situations, at an opportune time you'll want to be able to rectify whatever you can.

I was a big deal chaser for about fifteen months of my life. As I mentioned, I became intoxicated by a big deal. When I hit rock bottom financially, I realized that the only way out of that situation was to produce myself out of it. I had to perform simple disciplines over a long period of time.

Looking at my liability debt, I had three options. Option number one was bankruptcy. As a recovering alcoholic and addict, I realized I had reinvented my addiction; I had become money drunk. For me to rectify that situation, bankruptcy would just be another denial. Instead, I chose the old-fashioned American way – I produced my way out. I buckled my seatbelt, and I sat in a chair for the next twelve months, putting in fourteen- and sixteen-hour days doing what was required to overcome that situation.

If you're a recovering big deal chaser, this is the lesson you must learn. You don't want to just get out of debt; you don't want to just get out of the hole. You want to internalize the lesson so you don't continue to reinvent the same situation over and over.

The Breakthrough Factor

How many of you say on January 1st, *"This* is the year. This is my breakthrough year. This is the year that I arrive"? Unequivocally those statements could be true. But if you find yourself still procrastinating in July, then all you're doing is big deal chasing. All you're doing is stating the same thing that you did the last year, and doing the same thing over and over again.

Therefore, what is the breakthrough factor when you're a big deal chaser? How do you break through your procrastination? First, you have to recognize that you have issues with procrastination – and you've got to stop joking about it. Whenever I told people I was writing a new book called *From Procrastination to Production*, someone would invariably laugh and say, "Ha-ha-ha, I'll be the first one buying it." That person is laughing through their pain.

You must become objective. You must become aware of the pain you are experiencing, because in the middle of that pain is where you can find your passion, your pleasure, and your joy. You must look into the heart of darkness at some point and realize that a series of events created this identity you are living in. No matter where you are on your journey, no matter what city you live in, if you're living in denial, it's time for you to change. It's time for you to begin to let go. It is in letting go that you will find the light in the heart of the darkness. There *is* an end to every tunnel – the key is to find the light, focus on it, and create a practical plan to journey toward it, step-by-step, day by day.

The Long-Term Game

Perhaps you have dreams of becoming a millionaire, a six-figure income earner, a successful businessman or businesswoman, a philanthropist; you want to become a person of influence and affluence. However, if you're just sitting at home, if you're financially challenged, if you're procrastinating, if you don't have a vehicle to take you where you want to go, if you keep getting ready to get ready – at some point you have to get realistic. It's time to let go of being positive and become objective instead.

I see so many people attempt to take on three or four projects or businesses at once. This is just another form of big deal chasing. I recently had one of my clients tell me, "I talked to so-and-so, and they said that I could make a couple of thousand dollars in four hours a week doing this business."

I responded, "It's not going to happen."

She was taken aback, asking, "Why not?"

I said, "Well, let's take a look at your situation. First of all, you are married with children, and you have a demanding career. You have a daily commute back and forth from work, and you already have one business you're just starting to master. Why would you remotely consider taking on another business when you're just starting to break through in the business you already have?"

This is a very typical situation for so many sincere people. Fortunately, this talented young woman took a deep breath and said, "Yes, you're right." Like many of us, she became intoxicated with the big deal: "Wow, $2,000 a month, and I only have to devote four hours of effort."

I'm not suggesting that it's impossible at some point in your life to create a couple thousand dollars a month on four hours of effort.

But that typically won't happen unless you've mastered the emotions, the disciplines, and the habits of a particular vocation that you can now duplicate.

But you can't possibly win the game by big deal chasing. You can't sit at home wishing and hoping and trying. You have to commit, you have to decide, and you have to decide daily. Success isn't based so much on what you do, it's what you do daily. It's daily discipline.

How many of you have an exercise routine? Did you practice that simple discipline today? Do you exercise three or four days a week, rain or shine? Is exercise part of your daily habit? How many of you have some kind of discipline when it comes to your diet? Are you eating more raw foods? Are you eating more organic foods? Are you drinking more purified water? Are you releasing yourself from sugar, trans fats, and other foods that do not serve you?

When it comes to success, moderation is key, and so is having a method. Why? If you don't have a method, then you have a method of failure. It's vital that you employ a systematic approach to becoming successful. It just won't happen overnight.

Create Emotional Stability

If you see yourself in the profile of a big deal chaser, instead of always creating big deals, go after some smaller ones first. Create some smaller victories that can compound, that you can take some pride in. Instead of hitting a home run and swinging for the fences every time, just focus on getting on base. You'll begin to see some progress. Occasionally, look over your shoulder to measure the ground you've covered. You've heard the old adage, "Inch by inch, it's a cinch; yard by yard, it's hard."

Using the analogy of the tortoise and the hare, I used to be the hare. I couldn't wait to get to the finish line so I could get to the next finish line. I used to believe that being that goal-oriented was healthy. But I discovered that no matter what goal I had achieved, it was never enough *because I wasn't enough*. This is very common in big deal chasers – they seek success to prove to everyone else that they're enough. If you give a big deal chaser a compliment, they typically don't even hear it, because they're already on to the next big deal.

Emotionally, if you have high highs and low lows, you peak and crash, peak and crash, over and over. The key to success is emotional stability. If you have a less than favorable day, don't let it keep you from getting a good night's sleep. If you let it affect your sleep, you'll wake up with a headache because you were grinding your teeth at night. You'll wake up with the constant pressure that you've got to prove to the world that you're enough; you have to go out and conquer the world and be a big deal. I know a lot about this – I lived it.

I'll never forget the very first Mercedes Benz I bought back in 1984. I bought it from a very good friend of mine, and the reason I bought it (I know this now) is so that I could drive up in front of four- and five-star restaurants and nightclubs and have it valet-parked.

I have always been good at attracting money, but as a big deal chaser in my twenties, I attempted to buy friends and love with money because I wasn't enough. Every time I ran out of money, I seemed to run out of friends, and I'd have to reinvent myself in another city or another business because I would constantly burn bridges. My outlet for all of this angst was drugs and alcohol. I would have big successes and equally big crashes.

The successes would be so big that I couldn't possibly manage them because I was so self-destructive. I finally learned to let go. I realized that success is not so much about what I did – it was what I was becoming, what I was feeling.

Do you realize that you don't require money or success to feel good about yourself? You can feel just as good about yourself living in a small home as you can in a mansion. A lot of times those mansions end up being sterile and cold – they don't have the same feeling as a quaint little home with a human touch. And what good is a castle if you don't have anyone to share it with? What good is success if you don't have love in your life?

Now, I have also learned that while it's love that makes the world go 'round, money pays for the trip. So, in context of this situation, you absolutely, unequivocally deserve to receive and achieve whatever it is you feel comfortable and capable of doing. Just make sure that you're not doing it merely for the love of the money. Make sure you do it because you love yourself. Make sure it's about expressing your creativity. Make sure it's about who you are and who you are becoming. When you achieve success from this perspective, you don't have to be a big deal chaser.

You can still be a big producer, but be sure that you're not producing so you can reach a certain pin level or get some kind of merit badge. Even though you might not be the best, you can be *your* best – because being your best is much more important than being *the* best.

Being the best is overrated; there's always someone smarter, brighter, better looking, more talented, or more intelligent right around the corner.

Success Is Earned

While you don't have to hit rock bottom to be successful, we all love stories of people who lived in their car. They dug quarters out of their couch. They ate ramen noodles, or lived on peanut butter-and-jelly sandwiches.

I recently coached a client who entered the Miss Teen America pageant. No one knew she had been able to get that far because she was living in a car behind a Pizza Hut. Now that's the kind of discipline that breeds character. Going through character-building moments and overcoming the challenges you face gives you a great sense of pride – as well as a great sense of humility.

When you overcome an overwhelming situation that has hindered you and held you down, when you have actually had the courage to look into the heart of darkness and overcome an addiction, when you've come back from being destitute or in financial ruins, that in itself is one of the greatest rewards you can receive, because no one can pay you for the feelings you get from that sense of accomplishment.

Accomplishment is what you do through your physical and emotional effort. *Entitlement* is what you feel people owe you. You may deserve success, but you have to earn it. Success is applied discipline over a long period of time in a vocation you have an affinity for. If you're in a business just for the money and you keep avoiding the actions that will create the results you seek, perhaps you should take a good look at that vocation.

Have Big Goals, but Have Bigger Habits

In my experience, at least 90 percent of the people I've coached have bigger goals than they have habits. They have bigger expectations than they have skills. They start a business, expecting to make $10,000 or $20,000 a month in their first year. This does happen occasionally. But more often than not, the only people who realize this kind of success are people who have already paid the price somewhere else. Overnight successes are seldom, if ever, the case.

Just recently, one of my clients told me about her mentor who is achieving a multiple six-figure income. This mentor was in her late twenties, and it's tempting to think, "Wow, she just fell off the turnip truck and became successful." However, she started her entrepreneurial career when she was in her early twenties. She had eight years of experience already. This is similar to my story.

I got clean and sober when I was thirty-two years old, started my entrepreneurial career, and went through a series of ups and downs early on. It took me eight years to hit multiple six figures in a direct-sales network-marketing company. I wouldn't be where I am today if I hadn't gone through those eight years. During those years, I also went through two years of big deal chasing, ending up $100,000 in debt, absolutely at financial rock bottom.

More Heart Than Talent

Hitting rock bottom is overrated, I can tell you from personal experience. If you're there right now, don't despair, because you have the skill, you have the talent, but most importantly, you have the ability to tap into that emotional area called heart. You have more heart than talent, and that's what you must tap into.

If you don't have the heart, you're probably in the wrong place at the wrong time. But if you do have the heart, and you know you're in the right place at the right time, then it's your responsibility (i.e., the ability to respond) to recognize where you are and capitalize on it.

Luck is when opportunity meets preparation. Luck does not lead to success. I've met a few people who got lucky and inherited money, and they got just as unlucky and lost it. I've encountered a few people that were heirs to large fortunes yet felt so guilty because they didn't earn the money that they ended up losing it all. It's the same with many people who win the lottery – because they feel they don't deserve it, they have challenges using their newly found leverage to manifest continuing prosperity.

Intoxicated by Production

Here's the remedy if you are a big deal chaser: Instead of getting intoxicated by all your dreams, get intoxicated by production; this will absolutely serve you. Even if you are still out of balance in your life, at least you'll be moving forward. You can figure out how to become more balanced later. Your law of alignment will change if you become productive.

Focus on something productive. Focus on something that you have an affinity or an aptitude for, or a reward you feel you can accomplish. If you've started a new type of business, first master the basic skills that go along with your new vocation. If you want to be a guitar player, don't focus on being onstage. That might be a dream. Instead, focus on learning the chords. Focus on learning the notes. Focus on mastering the strings.

Success is a process. If you're not willing to devote two to four hours a day on a part-time basis to your future freedom, or six to ten hours or more if you're full-time, then you're probably delusional, and you'll end up in denial. The price of success itself is a privilege – and there is no price when you understand it's a privilege. Back in 2001, on a conference call, I said to Burke Hedges, author of the empowering book *Who Stole the American Dream?*, "Burke, I am paying the price." I'll never forget his answer. He said, "Jeff, it ain't no price; it's a *privilege* to do what we do."

Positive Characteristics of a Big Deal Chaser

Big deal chasers possess certain qualities that they can apply practically to create results. If you have a big deal chaser in your family or your organization, look for these qualities and affirm them. First of all, big deal chasers have natural, emotional, etheric energy, and when that energy is channeled, they have the ability to attract great people and form strong relationships. Big deal chasers are often good speakers. They're motivated, and they have charisma. They are often beautiful, charming, witty, and talented. When channeled properly, a big deal chaser can transform into a big producer.

Channel Your Energy

The movie *Wall Street* was all about big deal chasing. The character of Buddy in *Wall Street* was a classic big deal chaser. That movie had a great ending: Buddy wised up – he let go of being a big deal chaser.

Do you spend too much time dreaming? Do you spend too much time romancing how it's going to be in the future? There's a big difference between creative visualization and chasing big deals, between *idealistic* big dreaming and *realistic* big dreaming, between daydreaming and actual visualization. And that's the kind of separation that you begin teaching yourself to create.

The big deal chaser must come down to earth, and when they do, they hit rock bottom harder than any other procrastinator type. If you recognize yourself as a big deal chaser, the good news is that you *can* change when the pain is great enough. You might require therapy, counseling, or a twelve-step program. You might have to get a "real" job. You might have to pay back debts, creditors, and family members, but you can become realistic, specific, truthful, and honest. You can change your language and the words you use. You can learn to produce in time frames. And most importantly, if you're a big deal chaser, you can begin to love yourself.

If you're a big deal chaser, don't despair, because you have a lot of talent. You have a lot of charisma. You have a lot of energy. But it is your responsibility (i.e., you have the ability to respond) to learn how to channel that energy. You can learn how to channel that energy into production. This is not about forcing yourself. This is not about willing yourself to change. Changing is about being ready to become realistic, become objective, and realize that anything worth achieving is worth going through the process.

NOTES

4
THE CHRONIC WORRIER

As we explore the various types of procrastinators, you'll probably recognize yourself in every one of them, because most of us have pieces of all of the types within ourselves. We're all comprised of many different feelings and emotions. For instance, we all worry from time to time. We worry that we might offend someone. We worry that we'll say the wrong thing, or we worry that we won't know what to say. We worry about failing in our enterprise. But some individuals worry so much that it becomes chronic; it becomes an identity. I call this type of procrastinator **the chronic worrier**.

The chronic worrier has more deep-seated emotional challenges than any of the other procrastinator types. This type of procrastinator lives in the "what ifs." They love the familiar. They crave the predictable. They cling to the confines of "averagism." They are very insecure with new challenges that could potentially take them out of their comfortably uncomfortable zone.

Did you grow up with a worrying parent? If you are a baby boomer growing up in the 1960s, did you have a mother or grandmother that constantly worried, waiting for the other shoe to drop? If you are in your forties now, there's a high probability that your grandparents were born sometime shortly after the turn of the century. They went through the Great Depression. We can only imagine what it would have been like to live during that time.

Worry gets passed on hereditarily from grandparents to parents to children. Sometimes we worry so much that we don't even know what we're worrying about. Maybe you were told not to dream too big because you'd only be disappointed. As children, most of us heard many statements that caused worry. Worry creates panic. Panic creates anxiety.

Of all the procrastinator types, the chronic worrier usually has the most anxiety issues.

Characteristics of the Chronic Worrier

The chronic worrier is easy to spot; they're fidgety. Their energy is somewhat frantic. Their eyes dart around; they don't look you in the eye. They sometimes bite their fingernails, tap their pen, compulsively jiggle their foot, check the time, or choose any multitude of ways to express their nervous energy.

The chronic worrier has challenges changing, deciding, and committing. When you ask a chronic worrier a question, you'll hear a lot of "um," "ah," "well," and "okay." This type of vocabulary comes out of their mouth because they're very concerned about saying the right thing. They don't want to make a mistake. They don't want to offend anyone. They're afraid to get out of their comfort zone. They tend to have challenges getting started, especially in sales and marketing.

The chronic worrier has to process everything. This is the type of person that lives in their head. The chronic worrier gets locked into an identity, and they agonize about relationships. They have a challenge connecting with others. They tend to be commitment-phobic. In relationships, they are so anxious about choosing the wrong person that they don't choose anyone.

The chronic worrier emerges out of the most intelligent sector of our society. Even though they're very intelligent, many times their emotional intelligence is very low because they have no self-esteem. However, let me state again unequivocally: we all have the ability to change. Don't start worrying that you won't be able to overcome worrying!

Chronic worriers typically are very fearful and anxious. Their anxiety can often lead to panic attacks. Chronic worriers are very indecisive; they are terrified of making mistakes. This usually stems from past situations where they experienced a lot of judgment. Their indecisiveness is a control issue. They can't control the "what ifs" of life, but they can control staying stuck in their worry even though this usually leads to disappointment. They're very cautious, and they live for security. They don't like the unknown. They don't like the idea of risk for reward.

Chronic worriers can easily get caught in "the paralysis of analysis." They tend to become frozen where they are, thus missing opportunities and people that would allow them to move forward. Chronic worriers usually have challenges with selling – more challenges than almost any other personality type. They aren't able to just be in the moment; they have challenges being spontaneous or being intuitive. Chronic worriers have to know all the answers. This is the type of person who joins an organization, attends all the events, takes notes... but they don't *do* anything. Why? They're stuck in paralysis of analysis.

Chronic worriers come across as unemotional. They have a strong tendency to stuff their feelings. They attempt to appear as if they aren't reading a script, but in actuality they are very scripted. Chronic worriers often seem aloof; they tend to be loners.

Chronic worriers have a tendency to be depressed. Often a chronic worrier is misread as being negative, but it's more that they are indecisive and depressed.

Chronic worriers typically are prone to some of the most debilitating diseases. Chronic worriers are some of the biggest time wasters, and this always leads to disappointment. Disappointment over time wears out the adrenal system and the immune system. In addition, chronic worriers create lactic acid in their muscles or scar tissue that builds up in the neck and back. All this is due to chronic worry held in the body. However, the human body is one of the greatest machines ever made. No matter what has happened in the past, it has the ability to heal.

Chronically worried procrastinators constantly seek approval and are typically dependent upon others for insight, advice, and assurance. They rely on others who have more self-esteem, more self-confidence, and more self-assurance. They seek direction from people who are directed. Unfortunately, these types of procrastinators tend to be emotional and spiritual vampires. If you recognize this pattern in your life, you want to learn to let go of the necessity of being told what to do.

Chronic worriers tend to be the biggest "stuff" collectors. They have challenges deciding what to do with all the stuff that they hold on to, and then they have to decide what to do with all the clutter that doesn't serve them. If you walk into someone's office and it's overflowing with papers, boxes, and books, there's a high probability that this individual is a chronic worrier.

Why We Worry

What makes the chronic worrier worry? What is it that causes this situation? We aren't born worriers; we're born with a clean slate. Typically, though, somewhere during childhood, a series of events begin to form a mood that becomes a feeling, and that feeling eventually becomes an identity.

Chronic worrying, like any type of procrastination, is an *effect*. What is the underlying *cause?* For a chronic worrier, the cause is often is a neurotic person (possibly a parent) in their circle of influence that they couldn't please. This might come from being an unwanted child, or from being a child with brilliant parents who pressured them to duplicate that success.

One client of mine was a doctor who went to one of the finest medical schools in the nation. Even though he didn't want to become a doctor, he complied with his parents' wishes, got a degree, ran up medical school expenses that totaled over a quarter of a million dollars – and he proceeded to fail miserably as a doctor because it was a vocation that he had no aptitude or affinity for. He did all this to please his parents, but in reality he ended up resenting them. Eventually, he was so consumed with not making mistakes that he made a colossal blunder and was sued for it – all because he was in a profession he never wanted to be in. When I coached him later in life, after his quarter of a million dollars worth of debt and a lawsuit that didn't serve him, he shared that all he really wanted to be was a musician, and he was finally pursuing that.

Another client of mine, John, was an average insurance salesman. He had been able to achieve somewhere between $40,000 and $60,000 a year. When I met him, he was in the process of changing vocations. In every one of our coaching sessions, John would tell me all about all the "getting ready to get ready" he was doing. He was listening to CDs, he had attended a webinar, and he was going regularly to events, seminars, rallies, and conventions. He was surrounding himself with a circle of influence made up of exceptional and intelligent individuals. Through this circle of influence, he had attracted some of the greatest coaches in the world. Unfortunately, he was doing all this on liability debt. He had spent about three years getting ready to get ready, getting all of his ducks in a row. He used to spend hours writing and rewriting scripts. He never made a prospecting call because he had become so neurotically perfect that he couldn't produce.

During one of our coaching sessions, we finally uncovered the cause that drove his effect: he was an unwanted child. He was the last of eight children – and not only was he the last child, there were seven years between him and his next sibling. His mother used to say to him, "When I found out I was pregnant with you, I cried every night for six months." His parents paid very little attention to him; he really got left behind in that family. By the time John was thirty-five, he was a chronic worrier. In the year I spent coaching him, I had the absolute privilege of assisting him to turn his life around.

At this point, John isn't a millionaire, but he is no longer a seminar junkie. John is in the process of becoming a producer. He realizes that he doesn't have to be a superstar to be successful. Most importantly, what I assisted John to realize is that *he is enough*.

Intellectualizing to Exhaustion

If you recognize yourself as a chronic worrier, isn't it time to let go of this? Chronic worrying is really about control. Chronic worrying is an outer body experience about the "what ifs" of what might happen. The left side of your brain begins to process this kind of information to the point where you are not able to perform because what you will be able to do will never be good enough. You hold yourself back in jobs and business ventures because of the anxiety that you might not be able to handle the pressures of the outcomes. You start to intellectualize and emotionalize what will happen magically one day when you achieve success. You begin to talk yourself out of the success you don't yet have because you're afraid you might not be able to handle it perfectly. You might not be able to handle it logically; you might not be able to handle it emotionally. Suddenly you're so exhausted that you now have an excuse to shut down and procrastinate.

For ten years now, I have held workshops for thirty participants called Breakthroughs to Success. I've created such a safe environment that, during the course of the event, the chronic worriers forget that they don't have to be perfect. There's so much love and warmth in the room that it starts to break down some of those emotional walls, and some of that processing begins to get released.

Processing is when you think and intellectualize; instead of being in your emotional right brain, you spend a lot of your time in your logical left brain. You procrastinate in isolated areas that you feel you have to control, areas you rebel against. If changing identities, changing vocations, changing cities, changing careers, changing mates, and changing how you've been changing brings out a lot of anxiety, perhaps it's time to change your philosophy.

The way to change is to decide that you're sick and tired of being sick and tired. One of my favorite actors, the great Lee Marvin, was asked near the end of his life why he quit drinking. He said it was because the pain was great enough. When an interviewer asked Bonnie Raitt why she chose sobriety, she said, "Because life is precious when there's less to lose."

If you spent a lot of your time being perfect and disappointed, it's definitely time to change. Every single one of us has the ability to change the power of a decision, the power of a commitment. We all have the ability to move through the four phases of belief: impossible, possible, probable, and definite. At any given moment, you can move into definiteness of purpose. You deserve to let go of the exhausting energy that surrounds worrying.

Worrying as a Control Mechanism

I know a lot about being disappointed. I know a lot about worrying. I grew up with a father who constantly worried about pleasing other people. He was an exceptional coach, but unfortunately I took on some of his worry. Even though I didn't want to be this way, there were many times in my life when I have been a people-pleaser.

When I was absolutely at rock bottom at thirty-two years old, I was so chronically worried that I wanted to take my life. One of my biggest worries was that I couldn't go to sleep without alcohol. I would spend the entire day massaging my emotions, talking myself out of not drinking hour by hour. This was exhausting. It was so exhausting that I'd eventually give in and have that first drink.

It took me six years to get that first day of sobriety at age thirty-two. My first day of sobriety was so liberating – the tears just flowed down my face. In the beginning, I almost couldn't believe it. When I went to my first AA meetings, it was extremely liberating not to be in that kind of control all day.

I now have over twenty years of sobriety through the grace of God, but I'd be lying if I told you that I never worry, or that I don't try to control certain situations. But here's an affirmation that will greatly assist you, as it has me: "I never have a bad day, only a few challenging moments."

I'm regularly asked, "What is that one significant moment? What is the breakthrough factor?" In my own life, it was when the pain was great enough. I hit a bottom that was so deep there was no other way to go but up.

Keys to Letting Go of Chronic Worry

Any type of transformation requires awareness; if you don't understand why you do what you do, there's a high probability that you will continue to do it. Here are some healing modalities that can begin to assist you.

Loosen up your muscles. Start to see a chiropractor relatively regularly even if you don't have neck and back challenges. At least get an x-ray, or get yourself adjusted once a month to loosen up the muscles in your neck and back. If you are a chronic worrier, there's a high probability that you grind your teeth at night, or that you have low back pain. Many times your low back pain is connected to emotional feelings about receiving, asking, and deserving, and this is also connected to your finances. And if this describes you, definitely find some way to loosen up your body.

You can do this through physical or nonphysical adjustments. Explore different kinds of massage, rolphing, yoga, tai chi, or any type of martial arts type of modality that gives you the opportunity to practice some emotional discipline.

Begin to get out of isolation. Start to get out more, even something as simple as going and sitting in a mall and just people-watching for half an hour a day. Stop obsessing. Spend less time online. Take a walk. Get a dog or cat if you're alone, a pet that you can share some emotional space with. Join a networking group, a book club, or an exercise class. It really doesn't matter what you do, but find a way to share some kind of activity with someone else!

Develop new perceptions about yourself and about the way you perceive the planet and the world. Let go of your neurotic perfections and move into a practical application with perfection. Take a look at your past history. A lot of your chronic worrying may be due to events from your past. Do some visualization exercises. Build a dream board. Buy *The Robb Report* magazine. Start to dream again.

Let go of intellectualizing. Begin to live more from your heart, not your head. Instead of overthinking everything, learn to live fully today. Tomorrow hasn't even happened. Many chronic worriers get caught up in their own psychosis of "what if." "What if I succeed? What if I fail? What if this relationship gets serious? What if it doesn't? If I do this today, then_____ ... If I don't do this today, then_____..."

This type of internal dialogue goes on and on to the point where it becomes easier to do nothing than to do something, and yet this procrastination type will typically begin to worry about doing nothing just to have something to process! Let go of attempting to process life and allow yourself to do the best you can for today – believe me, tomorrow will come no matter what happens today and present you with a whole new set of experiences to learn and grow from.

Practice vulnerability. Practice saying, "Now that I've grown up, I give myself permission to be more vulnerable. Now that I'm grown up my vulnerability is my greatest asset, not my greatest weakness." I'm not talking about being so vulnerable that you get hurt. I'm talking about being vulnerable enough that people can connect with you. This means taking educated risks about being an emotional being and expressing your feelings about situations, not just your thoughts. Everyone may not agree with you, but I believe you will be surprised at how well people relate to you and choose to be around you once the "real" you is revealed.

Live in the present. Isn't it time for you to step into that space called the present? Living in the present is what will allow you to let go of procrastination. That's what will allow you to let go of your chronic worrying. All any of us can do is the best we can in any given moment using the tools we already have. Perfection is so overrated! When we live in the moment, roadblocks can become building blocks. How can we ever change if we stop growing? Every moment, every situation, is an opportunity to learn something new, expand our horizons, and change just a little.

The present moment is where we can let go of judgment and free ourselves to live life like a voracious child who just can't get enough.

Some Questions and Answers

Chronic worriers are full of questions. The key is to learn to ask *quality questions,* not obsessive, anxious questions. Here are my answers to those types of questions.

Q. "Can I really succeed in my enterprise?"
A. I'm not sure if you can make it, because you haven't even started. How can you ever succeed if you don't start? Let go of whether you can make it, and put more energy into what you do today; success isn't so much about what you do; it's what you do daily.

Q. "What happens if I fail?"
A. Even if you do go through some challenges, it's those very challenges that will provide you with life's lessons, that will give you experiences that will develop character, and that will assist you to develop a whole new personality.

Q. "What if no one buys from me?"
A. What if someone does? If someone does, then isn't that the ying of the yang you've created?

Q. "What if my family doesn't love and support me?"
A. If you're already stepped into entrepreneurship and they have jobs, there's a high probability that they think you're a flake anyway. You can't pick your family, but you can definitely pick your friends. If your family doesn't endorse you, if your family

doesn't love you, if you're disassociated in your family, there's always a great new circle of friends waiting to connect with.

Join businesses and groups where you can create that heartfelt connection. Toastmasters, BNI, network marketing, and direct sales are just some of the groups you can join. A twelve-step program can introduce you to some kindred spirits you require to create an emotional spirituality that may be missing for your life.

Receive the Rewards

A gentleman gave me a supreme compliment recently after hearing me speak. He said, "When you walked into that room, I could *feel* you!" That hasn't always been a positive thing. If you could have "felt" me twenty years ago, you would have felt my anger. If you could have felt me ten years ago, you would have felt my resentment.

Even today, I carry some of that resentment from being hurt, abandoned, and neglected. I still feel shame and guilt over some of the failures, ups and downs, and embarrassing moments I've created through my addictions. I dropped a game-winning pass in a football game when I was a sophomore in high school. I dropped the baton in a state track meet. I've done lots of things in my business life and personal life that I regret. I've alienated others and hurt their feelings. But when it's all said and done, I've learned to forgive myself. That's a permission-based exercise that we all deserve to experience.

If you're in a similar situation, there's no time like the present to let go of your chronic worrying. There are a lot of disadvantages to being a chronic worrier. You absolutely deserve to receive the rewards your brilliance can attract. You unequivocally deserve to receive the soul mate you are seeking. You definitely deserve to build that business model you've waited for; you deserve to *design* your life. You deserve to live your dreams, and the only way to do this is to let go and receive the rewards.

No matter what you've done, you can change. No matter what you've created, you can undo it. Now matter how stuffed your garage is, you can clean it out. No matter how challenging your finances are, you have the ability to overcome this situation and create prosperity. But if you don't change the way you've been changing, then you will continue to get what you're getting. And if what you're getting disappoints you, isn't it time to change your philosophy?

If you are ready to do that, congratulations and welcome aboard. You've stepped into a new league called the big league. Instead of being a chronic worrier, you are on your way to becoming a person of influence and affluence. You *can* be the person you've always wanted to be.

NOTES

5
THE REBELLIOUS REBEL

The next procrastinator type, **the rebellious rebel**, really hits close to home for me. The two procrastinator types that I identify with the most are the big deal chaser and the rebellious rebel. The characteristics of these two personality types have contributed to my tendency to procrastinate in isolated instances. What I have learned through my own growth and development is that the more we understand why we do what we do, the easier it is to change. Regardless of which procrastinator type or types you identify with most, you are traveling on the right path to understand yourself more clearly and change your behavior.

Characteristics of the Rebellious Rebel

The rebellious procrastinator exhibits passive-aggressive behavior. They say what they want people to hear, but they only do what they want to do. They may agree to something, but that doesn't mean that they will do what they say. They get their attention through creating conflict. They do more to create conflict than they do to produce.

Rebellious rebels often come across as hip, slick, and cool. They may look suave and debonair, and they may even come across like an amiable relater-type of personality. A rebellious rebel might appear to be a great giver. (This type of personality also shows up in another procrastinator type, the angry giver. The angry giver, the rebellious rebel, and the big deal chaser procrastinator type all have some similarities, but there are also distinct differences.)

Rebellious rebels look like they really have it all together and initially you might be envious of them, but the more you get to know them, the more you see that there is a lot of emotional chaos behind their shiny veneer.

I once had an employee that seemed very attractive, outgoing, and pleasant, but the more I got to know her, the less likable she was. The warm smile that I first saw when I hired her masked the fact that she had a very controlling mother. What she did was never good enough for her mother. Because of her underlying perception, this woman continuously created situations of conflict and control to fulfill the identity that she was living in.

Conflict and defiance is a big part of a rebellious rebel's identity. This keeps them busy rather than productive. Their defiance becomes their procrastination. Like the big deal chaser, they have entitlement issues. They don't refuse to do things outright; they simply don't do them at all. What they do is usually accomplished in a very inefficient manner in the midst of their rebelling. Being a nonconformist is great, but don't be such a nonconformist that you can't conform to your own success. Don't be so rebellious that you end up rebelling against your own success.

The rebellious rebel is very talented but lives by the law of entitlement. Their assets virtually become their liabilities. Often they are so talented that they don't want to practice when it comes to a sport. All they want to do is show up and play the game. Rebellious rebels don't feel like they have to engage in the emotional discipline, repetition, and experience that lead to mastery. They don't think they have to pay the price. They don't want to go through the process; they just want the payoff.

Rebellious rebels mask their low self-esteem with high self-confidence. They fall into the "look good, feel bad" category. Underneath it all, they are victims, living in denial, and they use anger to mask their low self-esteem. Once a rebellious rebel's anger sets in and they have created the conflict they are addicted to, they can now justify procrastinating. They brood and pout and exude a very hostile, toxic energy. When a rebellious rebel asks questions, it's with an underlying edge of anger and control. They usually interrupt other people before they even get their first answer. They love to cause scenes and conflicts.

Rebellious rebels have the potential to be very productive and often are neat and orderly. However, rebels stay stuck in the emotions of anger and resentment; they are easy to spot and easy to read because of how uptight, angry, and rigid they are. You can see this in the way they hold themselves. They are very toxic. They are very obsessive/compulsive, and within that obsessive/compulsive behavior is their passion.

Rebellious rebels tend to be full of anger. In addition to having strong addictive tendencies, rebellious rebels have the greatest tendencies to break down emotionally because of all the rage their procrastination creates. Their anger can cause cancer if held onto long enough. It can create MS or other debilitating neurological diseases. Rebellious rebels are constantly AATT (Angry All The Time), full of spite toward anyone who challenges their ideas, power, or authority. They get frustrated very easily. They fly off the handle. They like to make scenes. Anger becomes hate. Hate becomes resentment, and this creates a full cycle of holding onto procrastination. There is tremendous energy in anger.

If a rebellious rebel learns to channel his or her anger, they have the highest potential to become a producer; they become a force to reckon with, just like they were a force to reckon with in their rebellion.

I've lived much of my life in anger, going out of my way to create situations that would end up creating resentment. In fact, resentment is the emotion that has fueled me the most. I've done too much for people, setting them up in a position where they couldn't possibly fulfill the expectations I've created, which then allowed me to be angry and resentful, which then fueled the feeling that kept me stuck.

In the middle of all this chaos, drama, and anger is a juice, a fire, a passion – and many times this type of personality, if their passion is channeled or harnessed, can turn things around. I'm a perfect example. I've hit rock bottom a couple times; I've been a victim, full of anger, spite, and indignation. Fortunately, I finally got to the point where the pain was great enough, and I chose to let go and change.

Rebellious rebels are so brilliant that they become stuck in their own brilliance. Many athletes, entertainers, and artists are rebellious rebels and nonconformists. They can go through years, sometimes decades, between an artistic or creative endeavor that brings them success. They might create an inflated ego and feel they don't have to go through the process like others do.

Of course, in many ways, being a rebel is appealing. It's empowering to say, "I could never work another job again." That's great, but you must be able to produce. You must be able to create profit. If you have a nonprofit organization from the discomfort of your home because you're rebellious, your rebellion isn't serving you. If your rebellion is channeled into procrastination, then all you'll produce is disappointment and anger.

Rebellious rebels alienate people and then justify this by blaming others, which gives them a reason to shut down and be angry victims. They feel victimized and respond in oppositional ways. These are the kind of people you'll see in a restaurant berating the waitstaff. They perceive demands on their time and energy as threats to their individuality. A rebellious rebel may respond to this perceived threat with indignation or defiant acceptance, which once again leads to procrastination.

Rebellious rebels tend to be great starters, but usually average-to-poor finishers. They come on like gangbusters, and then they expect to coast. They avoid tasks they don't like, saying they are menial and unimportant. It's very common to see someone with a lot of skills and talent, especially in sales and marketing, to say, "Well, I really don't want to prospect. That's not really what I do. I'm so good that people will automatically buy from me. I can sell ice to an Eskimo."

Instead of taking the word "sales" seriously, turning it into the profession that it really is, rebellious rebels tend to be amateur salespeople who expect to sell based on entitlement and manipulation. There's a huge difference, however, between manipulation and persuasion. Manipulation is coercing someone to comply with you and do what you want. Persuasion is showing someone value and how they can benefit through the services that you're performing, which leads to WOO (Winning Others Over).

To really connect with people, we must be able to connect with ourselves first. If we are constantly angry with everyone else, we're actually angry with ourselves. This is usually because some violation put us in a situation and we haven't yet forgiven the cause that created the effect. We hold onto that situation, and then we justify everyone not liking us by alienating them. That way we can procrastinate. This is a description of a rebellious rebel.

Rebellious rebels are addicted to adrenaline. However, it's really not noble to walk around the planet saying, "I'm an adrenaline junkie." This type of procrastinator gets an immediate rush, an emotional high from not only creating conflict and drama, but also from how they will have to perform to resolve the crisis they have created.

A rebellious rebel has challenges with relationships and ends up sabotaging most of them. Even though they have some great qualities, their anger, brooding, and pouting often override those qualities. A rebellious rebel's long-term relationships pose serious challenges, because they ultimately antagonize and alienate almost every serious prospect. Potential mates are put off by their arrogance and insensitivity.

Rebellious rebels tend to use people by borrowing money. Of course, they plan to pay them back some day because they are so cool that their ship is bound to come in. The really hip, slick, good-looking rebellious rebels are the ones with the big ideas, the big talent, and they can often seduce other people into buying into their next big project. Then, if the big project doesn't hit a home run, the rebellious rebel has to find a new social group, a new town, a new city, or a new place to play.

There is another type of passive aggressive rebel: the weak-meek rebel. Women, especially mothers, often fit this description. They often become overweight, addicted to disappointment, turning to food for comfort. They tend to over-give so that they can be indignant and disappointed. They blame others when they don't get the peace they seek. They rebel against perceived authority and focus on blaming other people. Their self-protective attitudes repel other people so they can justify being disappointed, and then they procrastinate.

Rebels are typically pessimistic by nature. This undermines their inspiration to produce in a timely manner. They feel put upon, which gives them a right to rebel and then procrastinate. They also perceive themselves as misunderstood, people who shouldn't have to perform and produce like everyone else. They feel at the mercy of the bad guys. They have a warped sense of the world in many situations.

Positive Qualities of the Rebellious Rebel

The rebellious rebel's best qualities are their passion, their tonality, and their energy. Even if the rebellious rebel is toxic, it takes a lot of energy to be toxic. Even if they're really angry, anger channeled can move a mountain, can pick up a car, or lead a team to victory.

I'm a classic example of someone who used to be a rebellious rebel with a passive-aggressive personality, addicted to resentment. It's in my DNA. It's in my genes. It's in my cells. Even though I was able to turn my life around, I still procrastinate in certain areas. I still rebel in certain areas. I still cause conflict, and I still have resentment issues.

Take a look at Mike Tyson. In the past, he was the absolute role model for a passive-aggressive rebellious rebel. Look at Robert Downy, Jr., and all the situations he went through in his twenties and thirties, and notice how he's transformed his life as he stepped into his forties. He addressed his addictions, and suddenly his movie career started to come together. He's been out of the tabloids and living a pretty creative life the last ten years or so.

Many people are able to overcome their anger issues. I've seen many individuals channel their anger into religion, spirituality, business, athletics, and philanthropic causes. The good thing about letting go of your anger is that you can then teach someone else how to let go of their anger; you can show others the way out of anger and procrastination.

A Magical Process

It's time to take an objective look at the cause that creates the effect, an honest look at the heart of darkness. It's time to look in the rearview mirror and begin to put the pieces together of why you do what you do.

Forgiveness is always the beginning. Choose to forgive the situations that created the cause that now is the effect. Create forgiveness so you can let go of the people who abandoned you, who rejected you, who traumatized you. No matter what procrastinator type you are, it's your responsibility – the ability to respond – to understand and embrace the power of forgiveness. Forgiveness virtually can take you off the hook.

See if you can identify the cause of your rebellion. Take a hard look at yourself and begin to bridge the gap between your procrastination and your rebellion. When you can do this with any of the six procrastinator types, it's a real victory. The whole purpose of this book is to empower you to identify cause and effect and then be able to let go. When you begin to do this, suddenly a whole new group of people appears in your reality; you are awakened to a whole new set of circumstances.

It seems almost magical, but it's really creation on demand. When we create on demand, we attract to our reality a reflection of the way we feel and the person we are in the process of becoming. This is when people and situations begin to appear, seemingly out of nowhere, to edify the positives we see inside ourselves. It seems magical because we have become accustomed to attracting that which edifies the negatives we see inside ourselves until our journey of growth begins. As we grow it happens like this: We let go; we let God in. We let the people we deserve into our lives. We let go, and suddenly the type of person we have been seeking shows up without much effort on our part. It's synchronicity, it's synchrodestiny, and it can and does happen.

One of my clients said to me recently, "I was sitting in the airport on the way home from Breakthroughs to Success, and this guy came up to me and said, 'I don't know who you are, and this may sound off the wall, but I feel compelled to give you this book.' Later, an older businessman approached me and said, 'I don't know what it is about you, but I want to give you my card. Would it be possible for you to give me a call at some point? I just feel that you have something for me.'"

Maybe you're thinking as you read this, "That never happens to me." You're right, because the minute you say it never happens to you, that becomes your expectation. To experience this in your reality, you would have to believe that it is a reality. You would have to let go of attracting the people that don't serve you so you can continue to be angry and procrastinate, and you would have to be able to let some peace and prosperity in, to let people see some of the light behind your eyes, to see that goodness in your heart. It's your heart that people want to connect with.

Key Questions to Ask Yourself

If you find yourself rebelling and procrastinating, here are some vital questions to ask yourself.

- In the next two to five years, what do I desire to become?
- What process am I willing to go through so I can become the person I deserve to become?
- What am I really willing to give?
- What am I willing to receive?
- What am I willing to create?
- Why do I procrastinate?
- What is the cause of my procrastination?
- Why am I so defiant?
- Why am I so indignant?
- Why am I so impatient?
- Why do I resent people?
- Why do I continually set myself up so that I end up resenting people?
- Why does this consistently happen to me?
- Why do I attract these catastrophes?

- Why do I find myself procrastinating more than producing?

These are objective, honest questions that you learn to ask yourself over a long period of time. Anything worth achieving is unequivocally, absolutely, definitely worth going through this kind of a process.

I went through this very same process. I finally realized that nothing would give me relief except understanding why I did what I did, and I started to take a good look at my anger. I started to buy books on anger. One of the first books I ever bought was by Ronald T. Potter-Efron, called *Angry All the Time*. I discovered a book on forgiveness, one of the few books I've ever seen, called *Radical Forgiveness* by Colin Tipping. I began to realize how important forgiveness is. I started to look at the cause of my anger, and I began to understand that I had misread some situations that happened to me in my childhood. I started to realize that I was blaming the wrong people. I started to realize that for me to ever live in the land of freedom and promise, I would have to let go of some of the situations that kept me a victim.

Even though I had achieved sobriety, I came to the realization that I was now a dry drunk. About ten years into my sobriety, I learned that I had to learn a different way to live so I wasn't angry all the time. It wasn't my intention to be angry, but it had become my identity. I realized that I was proud of being a nonconformist, so full of pride that I thought rules were for other people.

Right now, take a deep breath if you recognize yourself as a rebellious rebel. Your anger is passion turned inside out. Your anger can be turned into creativity. You can begin to let go of your anger and begin to love yourself. Otherwise, how can you ever receive love?

Choose Collaboration – Not Conflict

Did you create a conflict today, or did you create collaboration? Were you warm and friendly, or were you angry, upset, and resentful? Did you generously tip someone, or were you upset that you didn't get the service that you felt you deserved? You have the ability to understand your own duality and begin to live in peace, in the present, in the moment, and in the now instead of holding onto the past that creates rebellion and nonconformity. There's nothing intrinsically wrong with being a nonconformist, but it's time that you channel that energy into productivity, passion, creativity, collaboration, and the ability to connect with people.

Rather than alienating people, it's time to connect with people. I recently had someone come up to me at an event and say, "So, is speaking and coaching all you do?" This person was putting me in a position where I would have to defend myself and validate my existence and what I do. But instead of falling prey to the rebellious rebel (because I'm a recovering rebel), I said, "What does that mean?" And the person said, "I, I, I, I… I didn't mean anything!"

I've learned as a recovering rebel not to take situations like this personally. I've learned not to set myself up for failure. I've become conflict-conscious, meaning that I'm able to spot conflict. This is a skill that you can choose to develop too. You can learn to recognize those who are attempting to draw you into conflict. You can let go of being right so you can be rich. You can develop the ability to step into the present and recognize when that situation occurs. Instead of stepping in another conflict, you step back, and your whole awareness, your whole energy, your whole being, and your whole presence begin to change.

When you live this kind of an inspired life, people want to be a part of it. If you are a rebellious rebel, you can rejoice in the fact that you can find an outlet for that angst, for that energy, that rebellion, that nonconformity, that juice, and that desire.

You don't have to be a victim. You don't have to be a procrastinator. You have the ability to become a producer, to become someone of influence and affluence. You can become a role model, a mentor, a messenger, an ambassador of change. You can become a pastor, a minister, an anything – whatever someone looks like to you who people look up to instead of away from.

NOTES

NOTES

6
THE DRAMA ADDICT

Now we'll take a look at **the drama addict**. This is the last-minute procrastinator, the type of person who believes they work best under pressure. They take pride in this, believing that it is noble to create all that frantic energy and adrenaline and then, at the last minute, save the day and rescue themselves.

Have you ever done something like this? You wait until your back is against the wall. It's raining, it's pouring, it's a tornado, it's a hurricane, it's a monsoon, it's a typhoon. You have no more money left in your bank account. You're emotionally and spiritually bankrupt, but suddenly you go into your closet and put on your superhero uniform. You look at yourself in the mirror, and you take pride in knowing that you have what it takes to overcome the crisis you've created. You dig deep into your soul; you overcome, you become victorious, and then, when it's all said and done, you're exhausted by all the energy you have exerted to overcome the very conditions you have created.

Or maybe you grew up with a drama addict in your household, someone who was always in the middle of a crisis or a meltdown. The drama addict can't conceive of any other way of life, and they delude themselves about how much energy this drama requires. They brag about overcoming obstacles, hurdles, challenges, adverse situations, and they are proud of the noble effort required to overcome these situations. In reality, they are chronic procrastinators who wait until the pain is great enough to perform because of how lazy and how entitled they feel.

In my own experience, I used to say things like "I'll succeed if it kills me," and it almost did. I lived with migraine headaches for eight years because of the pressure I put on myself. I learned later in life that pressure is an illusion. We create our own pressure, and we stay in that pressure in order to release all the cortisol that keeps us stuck and all the adrenaline it takes to conjure up those superhero feelings to overcome the situations we ourselves have created.

Drama addicts are one of the most destructive of all the procrastinator types. However, the light that shines within this procrastinator type is that they are highly creative individuals. It takes a lot of creativity to produce the kind of drama that many of us have lived in! There are many similarities between the rebellious rebel and the drama addict, but we'll examine some key distinctions.

Characteristics of the Drama Addict

The drama addict's ego continually attracts and creates drama, and it tends to weather the storms of crisis and chaos. Drama addicts are very responsible for the very drama that they create. They're addicted to their feelings, and they thrive on the adrenaline rush of saving the day under emergency conditions.

Drama addicts are either very meek and timid or they're hostile and energetic. Other people have to constantly take care of their personal and professional business while they pursue one distraction after another just to keep their life dramatic and entertaining. The drama addict lives in his or her own movie. They're always on the go, keeping in touch with family and friends, but seldom on time. They like to make dramatic appearances.

Drama addicts are codependent. Drama procrastinators are preoccupied with the adrenaline of drawing attention to themselves and getting others involved in their chaotic lives. They live in denial and seldom face into the way they waste time procrastinating and exhausting their energy in drama and chaos. The drama addict attracts people and situations that will constantly send them into crisis mode.

Now, that just defined the way I used to be. In recovery, I discovered that not only was I an addict, I was also very codependent. In other words, I could go into crisis mode and I could also go into rescue mode. I could be a drama addict, and I could rescue drama addicts – either way it fueled my self-esteem.

Drama addicts are dreamers. In the drama addict's personality, there's usually very little separation between sabotage and success. Drama addicts attract people and situations that constantly send them into this crisis mode. They bounce from one extreme to another – a high-high to a low-low. Even in high-high mode they can procrastinate, because here the drama addict starts to paint pictures. They romance the outcome. They see vividly and they're very creative; they have many similarities to the rebellious rebel. They're able to create drama with someone, or they're able to rescue that same someone from drama. The words *practical, methodical,* and *realistic* don't fit their vocabulary. They are lofty dreamers and extremely idealistic. They don't have the time to be realistic or practical. It's too boring.

Drama addicts live for disappointment. This is why procrastination becomes such a way of life for them, because by procrastinating they do not fail.

By procrastinating, they can end up eventually blaming someone else and justify not taking responsibility for their own feelings. They overlook the mundane, day-to-day routine aspects of life (i.e., paying bills, filing taxes, eating healthy, exercising). Drama procrastinators are not detail-oriented. They live in a constant dream state. They drop crisis statements like, "Oh, my life is over; I want to kill myself. I'm beside myself. How am I going to pay my bills?" They're victims starved for attention. By dropping dramatic statements, they not only attract attention from other people, but they gain a reason to procrastinate. They get intoxicated with how bad the situation is, and they operate from a very deep pain and pleasure principle.

When the pain is great enough, the drama addict sometimes can find a space where they are comfortable enough to let go. They go into a superstar mode where they overcome their challenges, but they never have balance when they're in this type of procrastination. They go from procrastination to production, procrastination to production, etc., and often their procrastination can last for years. They attract attention by appearing powerless and depressed. This gives the drama addict a consistent reason to procrastinate.

Drama addicts have very intoxicating personalities. Even though they alienate other people because of their drama, many of them have great people skills, and so they're able to persuade people to rescue them. (Remember, I speak from experience.) This type of person can baffle you. They appear to have the goods, all the qualities of success. They're the people who should be but aren't. Even though they're usually the most talented, the most creative individuals you know, they've often also been the most traumatized, the most wounded, and definitely the most broken.

The good thing is that, because of their creativity, no matter what state a drama addict is in, they *can* overcome it.

Drama addicts create a lot of resentment in their families and circle of influence. Drama addicts are very good at turning situations around so they can control other people's feelings, which then allows them to justify being a victim. When they are in victim mode, they typically begin to procrastinate. And in that procrastination, they can have a major meltdown; they might seduce family members or others in their circle of influence to rescue them or take care of them. After outbursts, blowups, meltdowns, or manipulation, they now have a reason to stay in bed the next day. They have a reason to pull the covers up over their head, avoiding reality. After all they've been through in their most recent crash, it often takes them days to recover and get back to some sense of production. It's not uncommon for them to take two or three days just to get back in the game because they hold onto their feelings, they hold on to the events. It is also not uncommon for drama addicts to appear puffy or swollen after one of these episodes.

The drama addict struggles with balance and consistency. Because of the drama followed by procrastination, they produce on adrenaline and frenzied energy. Their major challenge is staying consistently productive due to their addicted feelings that lead them to drama, then procrastination. They easily become exhausted and overwhelmed because of all their bottled up emotions. These are the feelings that keep the drama addict in drama. It's almost always a violation, either physical and or emotional, that creates their feeling of overwhelm. They went into an outer body experience during one of these episodes, becoming so overwhelmed that they have remained in suspended animation, holding onto and stuffing these feelings.

It's very common for the drama addict to end up either completely overweight or completely undernourished due to the duality and contradiction they live in. A drama addict might bounce from a weight gain to a huge weight loss. They don't know where to find the middle ground. That middle ground is what you're seeking to find if you identify with this personality type: balance, harmony, spirituality, reality, and objectivity.

Drama addicts go from one behavioral extreme to another. They're underachievers and underproducers. They brood and pout, and then they create more intense crises, dramas, and scenes to justify their victimhood. They have not learned the separation between being a victim and a victor. To create the intense pressure they thrive on, drama addicts procrastinate to the last minute – until the buildup is so intense that it requires a superhuman effort to even finish a task. They like to tell stories about the enormous effort it took to become exhausted. At the end of the day you'll often hear this refrain: "I'm so exhausted! You have no idea what I've been through!" or, "What I had to go through to get here! The traffic was horrendous." Their words are laced with drama. A lot of their conversation is about themselves.

Drama addicts are intoxicated with their own stories. This type of procrastinator's drama is attached to the stories they use to maintain their identity, which creates the excuse to procrastinate. Procrastination allows their low self-esteem to rule; it enables them to not fail. Drama addicts don't see this, though, because their stories become their identity. I have empathy for this type of procrastinator because all of them have been wounded, hurt, broken, traumatized by situations and events that have shaped their feelings into such an identity. Their feelings have become their mood, and their mood becomes their identity. Now they identify with being a drama addict, with being a drama procrastinator. They tend to create drama so that they can be the center of attention.

Drama addicts are very theatrical; they crave the spotlight. The movie *Sunset Boulevard* starring Gloria Swanson and William Holden tells the story of a classic drama addict, a fading actress who wanted to be back in the spotlight. She hadn't acted in years, spending those years hidden away in her mansion because she wasn't able to cross the bridge from silent film to talkies. She procrastinated for years, and then she created this big, dramatic event that led to a major outcome. Drama addicts thrive on pulling other people into their dramas. They thrive on getting attention from everyone else. They generate suspense, and procrastination is the tool they use to perform to their dramatic feats.

Drama procrastinators also tend to carry a lot of unresolved anger and resentment, creating blowups and confrontations. They slam doors, stalk out of rooms, shouting loud threats. Procrastination becomes the reason to blame others. The drama addict consistently points the finger at other people. This type of energy creates the high-high they unconsciously seek. They get a shot of adrenaline, and when it all blows over, remorse, guilt, and shame sets in, followed by a low-low leading to stabilization until the next eruption occurs. Between stabilization and that eruption, procrastination sets in.

Drama addicts often turn to alcohol and drugs to take the edge off of their unresolved feelings. This garners lots of attention from spouses, friends, and family members. Their behavior is not intentional – they are simply looking for an easy, painless way to release some of the emotional pressure they create and cannot escape on a day-to-day basis. They often convince themselves that they are chemically or hormonally imbalanced and will pursue every avenue they possibly can to find a cure – anything except to look inside and change. They run to doctors for prescription medication because of their ADD, their mood swings, their bipolar situation, and eventually they become addicted to pain pills – uppers, downers, whatever. Unfortunately, the drama procrastinator has the highest rate of suicide, because it takes a lot of energy to stay in this kind of state. It wears out their immune system and their adrenal system; it can lead to debilitating diseases because of how much energy they exhaust in this kind of modality.

Affirmations for Recovering Drama Addicts

Many years ago I created affirmations for myself that I began to use to neutralize my own drama. Here are just several of them:

"Struggle-aholic no more!"

"I'm tired of the drama. I am dropping the drama."

"I am a recovering drama addict. I'm a recovering chaos creator. I no longer require this drama."

"I am aware of other people's drama. I'm learning to become objective."

Ask yourself which emotion creates your drama – is it anger, hate, guilt, resentment, abandonment, rejection, or feelings of overwhelm? Next, recognize how this drama leads to procrastination, how procrastination leads to disappointment, how disappointment leads to guilt and shame, and how it all leads to a life of unrealized potential.

Develop an Objective Awareness

Covering this content, I know exactly what it feels like to create this kind of drama because it is so close to my soul. Here's a recent example. Someone no longer wanted to use my speaking services, and I held onto to this situation for a few moments, a few hours, even into the night – for the first time in many years I actually woke up in the middle of the night feeling all worked up over it. I woke up in a sweat, and then I realized how much energy I was giving to someone else.

You must develop an awareness about why you do what you do when you know that it absolutely, unequivocally no longer serves you. I went through this myself. I spent the last two years of my alcohol addiction in procrastination. I had a job, but I did just enough to get by. I barely made my quotas, yet I would drink myself into oblivion every single night. Every day, I would wake up with a hangover, and it would take a miraculous comeback early in the afternoon for the fog to lift. Then I would go into absolute overdrive and make up in the afternoon what I didn't do in the morning, becoming exhausted by 5:00 p.m. At 5:00 p.m., my drinking bell would go off and I'd repeat the pattern all over again.

If you have a lot of chaos in your life, it's time to let go of it one minute at a time. Take some time to objectively and realistically evaluate your situation. Did you create drama today? There's always going to be some measure of drama and chaos – that's life. But did you use drama and chaos as a way to get attention and eventually procrastinate?

If that is the case, begin to get real with yourself. Learn to become objective. You can change the way you feel. You can change the way you operate. More than anything else, if you are a drama addict, you require learning how to relax. Trapped in self-destructive cycles of excitement, adrenaline rushes followed by collapses, you'll never appreciate the energizing value that genuine peace of mind, the state of flow, offers until you consciously reinvent yourself to achieve it. This is exactly what I've been learning for the last twenty-three years.

If that describes you, isn't it time to step into your power rather than continuing to be powerless? When you start to understand this, you no longer give power to these feelings. Instead of being an accident waiting to happen, you become a person who's liberated. You become a person of influence and affluence.

Neutralize the Drama

We will have people that show up in our life to remind us of past events; no matter how advanced we are, we will always have some drama and chaos. The key is to learn to neutralize the feelings that create the cause so you can live in the effect. This requires autonomy (i.e., independence). The next time you feel yourself going into drama, see if you can catch yourself before you go over the edge.

Start by taking a deep breath.

To overcome drama, you first learn to spot it in yourself and then you can sense, feel, and see it in other people. You become a recovering drama addict. Instead of being a drama procrastinator, you become a productive producer. The opposite of procrastination is production.

Someone recently called me and began lecturing me on situations he perceived I had created. In reality, this person was using me as an excuse for his own lack of self-esteem and the challenges he himself had created. During this conversation, I started to feel those same old feelings, but before I went into full overreact mode, I was able to neutralize them before he seduced me into his drama.

Choose Your Words Carefully

Begin to change your language by avoiding overly dramatic language. One of the number one statements that I teach my clients to let go of is how tired they are, how exhausted they are, how worn out they are. Your unconscious mind sees no separation between fact and fiction.

Over my long career, I've learned to *rest* and not put so much energy into sleeping. I seldom wake up in the middle of the night the way I used to. I used to have night sweats. I used to toss and turn. I used require medication to go to sleep, anything to take the edge off. Peace has now become a way of life, and my energy has changed.

Words do not return void. The words that we speak become our reality. Isn't it important at this point in your life to begin to change your word choices? Speak into existence that you are not a drama addict, that you are not a procrastinator. You merely procrastinate in isolated areas where you perceive pain. As you identify the areas where you procrastinate, you will develop the awareness required to let go of the feelings that create the pain effect. Understanding the cause that creates the effect is the key to releasing your procrastination.

At the same time, realize that, no matter how good you get, there will be times when you procrastinate. Being perfect is overrated – being good is enough. When you realize that being good is enough, then you can become great. But if you have to be a superstar without going through the process, you will unequivocally set yourself up to be disappointed. And disappointment always leads to the modality of procrastination.

Tips for Dropping the Drama

Here are some insights about how to release the feelings that keep you creating the same situations over and over. If you identify with creating drama, which then provides you with an excuse to procrastinate, visualize what it would look and feel like to be a producer. What would happen if all your clutter and chaos began to drift away? What would it feel like to not have drama?

If you find yourself creating drama, chaos, and crises, imagine the toll it's taking on your body, your life, and on the people in your circle of influence. Visualize what it would look like if all the drama disappeared. You possess the ability to become a philanthropist. You have the ability to heal. You can develop the ability to teach and lead. You own the ability to create wealth.

Everything that you require is within you.

With all the creativity it requires to create all this drama, imagine the production you could create – imagine the lives you could change. Imagine what your life would look like if you begin to eliminate much of the drama. Ask yourself, "Am I ready to transform?"

Stress is an essential part of life. We're inclined to think of stress in negative terms like anxiety, pressure, or tension, but it also has positive connotations like excitement, intensity, and stimulation. Begin to look at stress as energy, the energy you have used to create drama, and channel that energy into passion instead.

Love what you do, and you won't procrastinate. Find something bigger than your problems. Find goals bigger than your challenges. Create and develop your purpose. Find something that motivates you. Live an inspiring life. When you begin to do this, you'll begin to play a whole different game.

Drama and procrastination take a lot of energy, but it's the same kind of energy that production requires. You can learn to turn this energy around. Instead of being a victim, you become a victor. Instead of being a loser, you become a chooser. Instead of sucking air, you become a millionaire. Instead of being exhausted, you're liberated. Instead of being intoxicated, you're inspired. Instead of being seduced, you're liberated. You're a highly productive person in society, creating results for yourself and others. You deserve to receive it all!

NOTES

NOTES

7
THE ANGRY GIVER

Now we'll examine two procrastinator types that really fit one identity: **the angry giver procrastinator** and **the overcommitted procrastinator**. In both cases, this procrastination identity is based on production. The angry-giver produces from a giving perspective, often with underlying anger issues beneath the surface. They tend to give, give, give, but their giving stems from a need for approval. They typically take on way too much in their role as a giver, becoming overwhelmed... and then they procrastinate.

Angry givers are so focused on taking care of everyone else that they neglect themselves, resulting in overwhelm and procrastination in key areas. They procrastinate about their health and fitness. They have challenges creating money for themselves because they're so committed to everyone else; they also have issues with guilt. It's very common for them to have issues with intimacy in their own personal life because they're so busy taking care of others. In a marriage relationship, they tend to give so much that they attract someone who doesn't receive, and then they feel resentful.

The highly productive, overcommitted procrastinator is very similar to the angry giver. They take production to an extreme to the point that they too have very little balance in their life. The overcommitted producer typically tends to base his or her whole identity on production. This individual doesn't usually come from a desire to *give* but from a desire to *produce*. Both of these procrastinator types tend to put in ten, twelve, fourteen, even sixteen hours a day. They'll do whatever is required to get it done.

Characteristics of the Angry Giver

Angry givers say yes to everything; they can't (and don't) say no to anything. They pride themselves on giving and serving. They give, and give, and give. They over-give to the point that they alienate the very individuals they attempt to serve.

Once I was hosting an event in Los Angeles and a very handsome young man came flying across the lobby. He said, "Let me take your bag for you."

I said, "That's okay. I'll take it myself."

He insisted, "No. No. Let me get it. It would be an honor." It actually became a wrestling match to the point I wanted him to get away from me.

He kept saying, "Why won't you let me take your bag?"

I finally said, "Because you're starting to upset me. Would you mind just moving on?"

He just didn't get it. His identity was so based on giving that it was practically offensive.

Years ago, I spoke to an organization that was based on serving. However, I began to notice a very interesting dynamic: While its members were great servers, very few of them were producers. They were so consumed with serving that a large percentage of their leadership never produced.

It was no accident that later the leader of this group and his entire team collapsed because there was no production. This is taking service to an extreme. There has to be a balance between serving and producing.

The angry giver's giving is often disguised; because of low self-esteem, their giving is really about control. This is an example of codependency. This type of giving allows them not to take care of themselves. Their whole identity is taking care of their kids, their parents, their grandkids. If they have jobs, they tend to take care of their superiors or the owners of the company. They are the servers of the world. If they're not taking care of someone else, they have no identity. This is often prevalent when there's a mom at home who takes care of everyone in a large family. When the last child leaves the home, that mother has to rediscover her identity. Serving themselves causes feelings of guilt, and this leads to inaction and procrastination.

There's nothing wrong with giving great service, but if service becomes your identity with no balance and very little production, then it's really an addiction. By now you know that addiction turns into procrastination.

Angry givers tend to over-give as a way to seek approval and recognition. Unfortunately, they never feel recognized and rewarded fairly because a large percent of the population won't reciprocate. Angry givers feel resentful because they're not recognized for their service. They brood and pout, causing drama and conflict because they are slighted. Their motivation in giving and serving is to be recognized.

Angry givers encounter major challenges when they move from being employees to entrepreneurs. They are so prone to give that they don't know how to produce for themselves. Their whole identity as an employee is working for other people and taking care of their job. I've coached thousands of people who were great employees but found themselves floundering as entrepreneurs. Typically, this type of person spends a large percent of their early entrepreneurial career getting ready to get ready – i.e., procrastinating. They always *seem* to be busy. They listen to calls. They attend webinars. They get trained. They go to events, seminars, rallies, and conventions. They do everything but produce.

Angry givers overcommit to their training; they become seminar junkies. They might go to a Tony Robbins event, followed by a Jack Canfield event, followed by a Mark Victor Hansen event, followed by a Golden Mastermind event, followed by another speaker's event. While they get great training that is meant to propel them to success, what they're really creating is a nonprofit organization from the discomfort of their home. Creating a profitable organization from the comfort of home is the dream; it is the romance – however, this creation requires application of knowledge gained in the form of production. Without production, procrastination takes over – thus the discomfort, thus the nonprofit.

The overcommitted, angry giver tends to not have a life. By over-giving, overcommitting, and overdoing, other areas of their life fall apart. They become so overwhelmed by the many obligations they take on that they end up neglecting and procrastinating about other important areas of their life.

Overcommitted givers allow their careers to consume them; they have no identity other than their profession. Relaxing is out of the question because they have so much to do. Guilt is a driving force in behind their busyness. They are too busy to relax… too guilty to slow down… too busy to have a relationship… too guilty to take a vacation… too busy to visit their relatives. Even productive givers neglect areas of life that will bring them joy: happiness, peace, relaxation, and – most importantly – love.

It's very common for this type of person not to be in a relationship because their career becomes their relationship. They develop a love-hate relationship with their career. They love what they do, but they take on so many roles that they get overwhelmed and eventually they end up resenting what they do. At this point, their production starts to fall apart, and they end up being merely busy. They end up procrastinating about having a life. They feel trapped in busyness and producing, not allowing themselves any time for enjoying life and relaxing.

Angry givers are easily seduced into saying yes when their intuition is telling them to say no. People in the angry giver's circle of influence know they can count on them because they are so dependable. "Can you run an errand for me?" "Could you possibly take me to the airport?" "Is there any way that you can loan me some money?" The angry giver hears them say, "I've been through some ups and downs, and it would really be awesome if I can seduce you into giving me money that I will never pay you back so that you can feel disappointed and eventually resentful, and thanks for the whole situation." Later, they resent the fact that they couldn't say no.

Angry givers can appear highly productive, but they are really busily overwhelmed. Their workload continues to pile up. They begin to miss deadlines and appointments. They overbook, overschedule, are continuously late, fall behind, and forget important information. This leads to a more undetected kind of procrastination. It is common for an overcommitted giver's life to fall apart in many areas.

I once coached a gentleman who had a job but was in the process of becoming an entrepreneur. His father made him the executor of his will, and then proceeded to demand much of his son's time. My client began spending three to seven hours a day just going through all of his ninety-year-old father's paperwork. Now, if this only lasted a few weeks, it would have been understandable, but this had gone on for years. Instead of being productive and running a business, my client spent almost all of his time taking care of his father. To this date, his father is still alive, well into his nineties and very healthy.

Angry givers typically don't take proper time to eat properly, instead consuming fast food and foods with trans fat, sugar, and caffeine. Exercise is often put off because this is an area that requires commitment, as is proper nutrition. "I just don't have the time. There's just nowhere to fit it in. My plate is so full that there's no way I can exercise. I realize that I'm carrying 240 pounds on a five-foot-eight frame, but you don't understand. I have so much to take care of. I can't possibly change my diet. I just don't have time. I can't plan ahead. I can't pack a lunch. I have no time to prepare anything for myself. I have to grab what I can and eat at my desk." Angry givers feel taken advantage of in situations that they themselves have created.

The angry giver has an inability to delegate due to perfection. Angry givers have to do tasks perfectly, and because of their inability to delegate, it typically takes them a lot longer to do what is required. Early in my entrepreneurial career, I hired one of my very first employees – a brilliant young man who showed lots of potential. In the beginning, I was easily seduced by his commitment. After a few months of watching him perform, it dawned on me that the time that he was giving me was very ineffective. Even though he was staying very late and telling me how committed he was, it was taking him a lot longer to finish tasks than it should. Eventually I had to let him go. While he should have easily finished his tasks by 5:00 p.m., he would end up staying until 9:00 or 10:00 p.m. He obsessed about certain situations. I wasn't requiring this, and in fact, his workload wasn't all that heavy. He spent way too much time overanalyzing in a paralysis of analysis. He would do things that I didn't ask him to do and then neglect the things I did request, feeling resentful that I would call him out on those situations.

It's very common for an angry giver to give more than is required and then procrastinate on doing what's actually important. This often shows up in their body. The angry giver tends to gain physical weight because of how weighed down they become in their overcommittments and their lack of discipline. Over-givers tend to overstuff themselves; they also stuff their feelings of hurt and resentment. They stuff their feelings with pills and alcohol, but primarily with food.

Angry givers have trouble with balance. Instead of overstuffing themselves, it's not uncommon for them to go to the other extreme, neglecting their health and becoming extremely thin because they deny themselves joy, nourishment, and relaxation.

They are so productive that they don't have time to enjoy their success; they always have their sights on the next goal or accomplishment. They never seem to have enough because *they* aren't enough.

Angry givers often take on service-oriented careers – counselors, healers, medical professionals, etc. Then they have challenges charging fees because they are conflicted about receiving. They give great service, but there is an incongruence between attracting clients, keeping the business going, and getting paid. They might have challenges collecting. I have coached talented contractors who ended up going bankrupt because they couldn't collect on their invoices. They did great work, performed great service, delivered great value, but they had tremendous issues in receiving compensation for the value they provided.

Most of us have grown up with the idea that it's better to give than to receive. Why is there so much distance between receiving and giving? Why isn't it great to do both? If this is something you struggle with, this series of affirmations will assist you:

Now that I'm an adult…

- I'm getting comfortable with giving *and* receiving.
- I am able to develop balance in my giving and receiving.
- I'm getting comfortable with becoming a great receiver.
- I'm feeling better about myself and about asking for what I deserve.
- I'm capable of asking for what I feel I have accomplished.

The angry giver may have been forced into a particular role as a child. I had the privilege of coaching a one-time tennis champion. She had been the champion of city tournaments in a large metropolitan city throughout her teenage years. One of her biggest challenges was being able to receive, and she put an incredible amount of pressure on herself. I discovered that, after high school, she tore her ACL, effectively ending her tennis career. She was able to get a college scholarship to a minor university, but she never excelled the way her parents wanted her to. When she graduated from college and was not able to play professionally because of the injury, her parents were extremely disappointed in her. Her father let her know that he felt he'd wasted his entire life savings so she could be a professional tennis player and take care of the family. As an adult, she felt obligated to pay her parents back for all the money they had spent on her. During our coaching sessions, I was able to empower her to exercise forgiveness and let go of the resentment she felt for having to take care of her parents.

I have coached countless clients who were forced into law school or medical school even though they really wanted to be artists, athletes, or musicians. I've coached several doctors that never wanted to become doctors. Instead of following their true passion, they were forced into careers their parents chose for them. One of them filed bankruptcy at age forty because he just didn't have the passion to run the business and thus let the business run him. His business eventually got run into the ground.

The Produceaholic Procrastinator

A subtype of the angry giver is the produceaholic procrastinator. That sounds like a contradiction, doesn't it? We don't usually think of a producer struggling with procrastination, but read on.

The produceaholic becomes overly committed to his or her own success; production has become their identity. They become so successful that success becomes their identity. They are so driven that they avoid other areas in their life – specifically intimacy, spouses, and immediate family. Even though they may get standing ovations on the stage, often they feel very empty when everyone's gone because they have no one around them to cheer them on. Success has become their identity. Money has become their identity. But when the success or the money goes away, their identity disappears too.

Now, I will be quite candid with you – I have found myself in this situation many times. I've been just as guilty as some of the produceaholics that I have met and coached in my career. These days, however, I'm giving myself permission to spend less time producing and experiencing more intimacy with my loved ones.

I used to feel guilty taking vacations. I used to procrastinate about having a life. The key to overcoming this situation is realizing that success is worthless if you don't have anyone to share it with. What good is money if you don't have anyone in your circle of influence? I have watched many people turn a business into an addiction. I'll be the first to admit that this has happened to me a time or two, and there are times that I still wrestle with this. Early in my career, I would produce all day late into the evening, and then before I'd go to bed I'd read personal development and self-improvement books.

To develop balance, I'll let you in on a little known secret: I love to read fiction. I love fiction because it allows me to escape.

Over a two-year period, I read every Louis L'Amour western written, and these were some of the most enjoyable moments I have spent. Initially, if I was on an airplane with my employees, I used to be too guilty to let them see me reading fiction. Finally, on one flight I just came clean and said, "Hey, fellas, look at this. This is called *Last of the Breed*. It was one of Louis L'Amour's last books. And this one's called *The Haunted Mesa*; it's one of the greatest spiritual books ever written. It's an awesome book, even though it's fiction." I love fiction – crime fiction, war fiction, and historical fiction.... I enjoy the History Channel, DVDs, movies, experiences, and travel.

I have a collection of classic cars. For years, I just let them sit in the garage, but now I've learned to be able to take one of my classic cars out late at night, put the windows down and feel the beautiful California air. What good is having a classic car that you dreamed of if you never drive it? It's time to smell the roses.

My wife is an avid equestrian with two beautiful horses, and it empowers her to create the time to ride them four days a week. Each year, she attends several horse shows where she rides competitively. She comes home from these experiences absolutely glowing as she relays her latest progress and breakthroughs in her riding. It is gratifying to me to see that as I create more balance in my life, it is opening space for her to enjoy her passions without guilt.

I used to hate the word balance. I used to cringe when someone would talk about balance; I would go into fight or flight. I'll never forget the time that two women picked me up in a car once on a way to an event. They asked me, "What do you do for fun?" I was baffled. What the hell was fun? I hadn't had fun since the late '70s. "I'm a producer. I produce." I really did say this, and I look back now and laugh. I know they thought I was a freak, and they were right because back then that was my whole identity. Being a produceaholic has cost me relationships in many areas of my life, but over the last several years I have learned to let go of control.

Taking Time for YOU

If over-giving, overdoing, or over committing has become your identity, it's time to take a good look at why you do what you do.

- When was the last time you took a vacation?
- When was the last time that you actually gave yourself the luxury and the latitude to take a little time off and devote some time to yourself?
- When was the last time you pampered yourself?
- When was the last time you did something for yourself?

It's time to let go of the guilt and begin to understand that becoming a highly effective, productive person requires some balance.

Recovering Angry Givers and Free Enterprise

If your whole identity has been based on taking care of other people and suddenly you enter the world of free enterprise, you might be walking away from your job mentality and your tendency to take care of everyone for the first time in your adult life. If you are building a leveraged enterprise that requires the ability to lead a team and develop a sales force in order to be able to get paid through multiple levels of other people's efforts, this requires bringing a lot of people into your circle of influence.

The failure rate is extremely high, because most people have been seduced into trading time for dollars.

If your whole identity has been serving, giving, and taking care of other people, there's a high probability you'll feel overly responsible for your team's success; you'll start to feel guilty when individuals fail, and you'll use that guilt as an excuse to procrastinate. When you bring people into an enterprise, it's not your responsibility to make them successful. If you take on that role, you'll set yourself up for disappointment. You'll feel resentful that the people who joined you failed, even though that failure had nothing to do with you. The real reason individuals fail in free enterprise is that they don't stay in the game long enough to master the life skills, the habits, and the mindset to become successful.

America is not only the land of the free; it's the land of the broken. A large percent of the population is challenged financially, physically, and emotionally. They have more liabilities than they have assets. They're not prepared to succeed. And if you are a recovering angry giver, you must understand your role in mentoring people, in facilitating transformation. It's never about *you*; it's always about *them*. You have to flip the situation around so that what you do is mentor, lead by example, facilitate, direct, and assist people to success, knowing their success is not about you.

When it comes to being able to mentor others, it's not just about giving and serving. It's about leading by example. Are you being a healthy example? Are you doing what you ask other people to do? If you're not, then you're just taking a walk. Instead, *devote your energy where it's deserved, never needed.* Time is your most valuable commodity. Eighty percent of your time should be devoted to producing. The other 20 percent of your productive time should be spent on mentoring, developing, assisting, and starting people off on the right foot.

Angry givers flip this around so that 80 percent of their time is devoted to helping, rescuing, and saving. If this has been your pattern, you are probably so disappointed, so exhausted, and so worn out that you don't remotely have an opportunity to succeed. You must develop boundaries. When it comes to time, recognize how valuable yours is and learn to say that two-letter word: No.

Keys to Becoming a Healthy Giver

If you see yourself in the profile of the angry giver, there are some specific keys to let go of this identity once and for all. Before I share them with you, here is an affirmation I created to assist myself that you might find valuable too.

More production; less effort.
More money; less production.
More money; more time to enjoy it.
More prosperity; more opportunities to dispense it.

Learn to limit your time by determining its value. You can learn to let go of your tendency to over-give and turn your time into value. Being an entrepreneur requires learning how to devote less time to more people. If you want to create more value through your service, you have to learn how to serve more individuals more quickly, and the way to do this is by not spending so much time taking care of everyone.

When I started to build large sales organizations all over the world, I learned very quickly that I couldn't possibly take care of everyone. If people wanted my time, it was up to me to place the value on it. If I let others determine the value of my time, they would take up my entire day. Learn to limit your time. Teach people how to converse with you. Tell people up front how much time you have available. "Hey, Jim. You just caught me between a call. What can I assist you with in the next two minutes?"

When someone goes into what I refer to as a drunkalog, you have to be able to cut him or her off diplomatically. You can do this by using their first name. "Steve. Steve." "Steve, specifically, what can I assist you with in the next two minutes? Steve, I'm just about to step into a meeting." If Steve begins to tell you a story, you can say, "Steve, do you have a question?" I take questions in large events all the time, and invariably people want to tell a story. If you're an angry giver, you must learn to be empathic, not just sympathetic. Sympathy is when you take on someone else's pain. Empathy is when you feel another's pain, massage it, and assist that individual to a result.

Know the difference between priority and demands. Priorities are events and situations that are personally important to you and that only you can accomplish. Priorities are personal. Demands, on the other hand, are events and situations that are important to someone else but require your time.

Monitor how long it takes you to finish projects. Do you overanalyze? Do you overestimate? Do you overdo and spend too much time on perfection that leads to procrastination?

Recall situations and events that you truly wanted to experience but never got around to because of your guilt with relaxation and joy. Take some time to smell the roses.

Instead of being a producer, become a relaxer. Become a relaxed producer. During this year, plan at least a three-day vacation. Take mini breaks. Instead of being consumed with production, focus on results and the time required to get those results. Develop the ability to produce more with less effort, and then spend that valuable time with your loved ones, the people who really deserve to feel your warmth, your spirit. Learn to put the same energy you put into serving, giving, and producing into relaxing, because you unequivocally deserve to receive it all.

Give yourself the luxury and the opportunity to create some new experiences for yourself. Go to more conventions. Attend a concert. Visit a museum. Buy a movie on DVD – and take the time to watch it. Develop a new hobby. Take a vacation. Walk your dog more. Spend more time with your loved ones.

Before going on to the next chapter, pick up the phone and call someone you haven't talked to in a long time. Send someone an email. Write a *real* letter. Reach out to someone on Facebook or Twitter. Most importantly, enjoy spending time with yourself. Live in the present and really let go. Let God. You deserve to let others serve and produce for you the way you've served and produced for them.

To Do for ME:

_____

_____

_____

_____

_____

_____

_____

NOTES

NOTES

8
THE RECOVERY PROCESS

So far, we've covered the six procrastinator types, we've identified what causes procrastination, and we've touched on some of the ways to overcome procrastination. In this chapter, we'll explore in more depth how to let go, transform, and truly become a recovering procrastinator.

Identify Your Procrastination Points

You are not a procrastinator; procrastination has been a false identity that you've adopted. Procrastination is only your identity if this is what you continue to tell yourself. The identity of procrastination gives you the justification, the validation, and the excuse you require to stay stuck.

However, if you are reading this book, you are someone who has decided to go from being a procrastinator to becoming a recovering procrastinator. Congratulations! This is the first step in your recovery. Just like a twelve-step program, there are multiple steps involved in letting go of procrastination. It all begins with a commitment and a decision – and most importantly, with awareness. This requires coming to terms with the areas that you procrastinate. Remember, you procrastinate to 1) control a situation and 2) to rebel against a situation.

This is a recovery process. You won't be consistent overnight. You will go through ups and downs, but don't give up, and do your best to be objective as you go through the process. Continuously seek improvement, and remember to look at the whole picture.

The first step is to admit that you have an issue with procrastination. The first step is saying, "I am a recovering procrastinator." With this realization, you can now begin to address the cause.

Step two is becoming aware of why you procrastinate. This begins by catching yourself in situations where you have a tendency to procrastinate. This allows you to first become aware of and then neutralize the feelings that lead you into procrastination. Then you can move from intent to commitment.

Overcoming Overwhelm

A major contributing factor of procrastination is getting overwhelmed. How do you overcome this? You move from denial to awareness. Denial is putting the blame on someone else. Begin – just begin – to clean out one corner of your life at a time. You can't do it all overnight. You have to take one bite at a time, one breath at a time – otherwise you'll stay overwhelmed. Begin to take responsibility for what you do and why you do it instead of validating and justifying your procrastination and the issues it causes. To change, you begin by not putting things off as frequently.

The more you understand why you do what you do, the greater the opportunity for you to neutralize the feelings that lead to denial. Denial leads to disappointment, disappointment leads to guilt and shame, and these are all components of procrastination. Procrastination always begins in your thoughts and feelings, and it is manifested in your self-talk.

Become Action-Oriented

As I was getting ready to board a plane to Atlanta recently, I encountered an exceptional flight attendant. A passenger had left a bag on the airplane. The gate agent was making a big ordeal out of the situation, trying to prove the passenger wrong. The gate agent continued to tell the passenger how difficult it would be to retrieve the bag, how he'd have to contact customer service, etc.

Suddenly, the flight attendant who was scheduled to be aboard that plane for my flight asked the passenger what the situation was. She calmly said, "I'll go get it." And that's exactly what she did. She walked on the plane and a few minutes later came out with the bag. Up until this point, there was a high probability that the gate agent would have delayed the whole flight because he had to be right; he was more concerned with proving the customer wrong than creating a result.

On that flight, I continued to observe the way this flight attendant operated. She was action-oriented. I found out that she had been a real estate investor since 1993 and the only reason she was a flight attendant was for the travel benefits. During her full-time career as a real estate investor, she also had a full-time career for over thirty years as a flight attendant. Here is someone that's a producer, not a procrastinator.

There was another flight attendant on board who was completely the opposite. We started talking, and she asked me a little bit about my coaching. When I told her what the investment in herself would be to hire me as her coach, her response was, "Oh, wow, I can't believe how expensive you are." That was her self-talk. This illustrates the difference between a producer and a procrastinator. Procrastinators find reasons not to do; producers find reasons to do.

To eliminate procrastination, you must live in the moment. You must be in the present. The time of your life is "now o'clock." Develop an awareness of time – learn to borrow time, leverage time, create time, and use time. Become action-oriented.

Create changes because you want to change, not because you are forced or are threatened. Begin to feel that juice, that internal energy; recognize that you're starting to feel different. Begin to feel that electricity. You're starting to feel a new sense of purpose, a belonging. You're beginning to feel connected. Most importantly, you're beginning to operate from a spiritual level. You're beginning to let go and let God. You're living in that space called "infinite intelligence." You're starting to say, "I am." You're starting to say affirmations like, "Now that I'm grown up, I am comfortable receiving money. Now that I'm an adult, I feel comfortable being the person that I've always deserved to be." You'll discover that when you start to operate in this space, procrastination isn't nearly as prevalent.

Live in the Solution

Procrastination is based on controlling an illusionary outcome. You can't control an outcome in the first place, but the reason you procrastinate is mistakenly attempting to control an outcome that you can't control. While this is contradictory, we can control disappointment, and we can control not failing. We can control the conversations that we never have. We can control being right. However, control always leads to disappointment. It leads to the pain of regret.

Tiptoeing quietly through life and arriving at your grave safely is not going to get you to the Promised Land. You must change; you must begin. Many first time entrepreneurs face this dilemma as they attempt to change a vocation, which often represents changing their identity. It is common for procrastination to begin very early in an individual's entrepreneurial career because their left brain kicks in, and they tell themselves, "I've got to get ready to get ready. I've got to have all my ducks in a row." This can go on for days, weeks, months, and even years.

You can't create results without action. You can't create results without production. You can't create results without being in the game. If you sit on the bench, all you'll collect is splinters and disappointment.

To overcome procrastination, you have to have a strong awareness and an even stronger reason to change. You have the ability to transform and change, but you must develop reasons that are bigger than your problems. If you look at how overwhelmed you are, you'll continue to experience overwhelm. But instead, if you look around and see the clutter, the chaos, the drama, the debt, whatever the situation is, and you decide to find a solution, you will overcome it. Winners always find a way. Average people always find an excuse.

I hope that, in these pages, you can feel the energy that's radiating through me, because I am very passionate about assisting people with releasing and letting go of procrastination. Procrastination is the thief of our society; it's the thief of our economy. It's why people go bankrupt. Many individuals give their home back to the bank because, quite frankly, they take the easy way out. They find ways to live in the problem rather than live in the solution.

Listen to Your Words

The more you catch yourself using words of hesitation and indecision, the higher the likelihood of change. This type of awareness accelerates the process. This requires attention to detail: paying attention to you words, actions, thoughts, and feelings. Become a master questioner. (On my website, I offer a ten-CD set called *The Psychology of Asking* which covers how to ask bigger and better questions.) Regarding procrastination, begin to ask yourself:

- Why am I procrastinating?
- Why did I avoid perceived pain?
- Why did I say what I was going to do such and such, and then not do it?

At this stage, there can be a conflict emotionally. Your old self-talk will try to talk you into procrastination because it is a familiar identity, one that will keep you from perceived pain. Once you commit, decide, and determine that you will not be denied, the wrestling match begins, especially early in the journey.

This is a one-day-at-a-time shift. If you try to change everything all at once, you'll get overwhelmed, you'll shut down, and you'll go right back into procrastination.

"God, grant me the serenity to accept the things I cannot change, the courage to change the things I can, and the wisdom to know the difference."

This little serenity prayer has brought me many moments of peace, many moments of stillness, and it is very appropriate to overcoming procrastination.

I highly recommend reading *The Power of Now* by Eckhart Tolle. This book goes into great detail about the ego, the left brain, the pain body, and perceiving pain or pleasure. Your unconscious will do everything it can to move you away from perceived pain, your ego will do everything it can to keep you stuck in your perceived pain, yet your right brain will do everything it can to take you into pleasure. We go to great lengths to avoid pain, even if that pain is just an illusion.

The Pain and Paralysis of Regret

You will relapse back into the familiar if you are not aware of *why* you do *what* you do. Don't be too hard or judgmental on yourself – never forget that you are human. You require peace and approval, not condemnation and judgment. Give yourself credit for some of your victories.

When it comes to letting go of procrastination, the greatest paralysis is regret. Regret is painful because you waste your time and deplete your energy going over and over the past instead of living in the present, living in the solution. It is a waste of time and energy to fixate on past relationships, jobs, careers, people, and events.

By focusing on regret, you avoid changing habits and patterns. Regret is easy; regret is familiar. Regret can become an identity.

On the other hand, transformation is challenging. The most difficult part is the initial letting go of control. Regret is mourning a loss; it's holding onto the past. The pain of regret is debilitating. When you let go of regret and live in the present, you are able to change your perceptions and feelings about a past event. Don't let your regrets become your excuse to continue procrastinating. Spiritually enlightened, prosperous people don't stay stuck in the past by continuing to repeat what they regret. Study your regrets, and start to realize what a negative payoff you receive by living in them.

Ask yourself, "What is my payoff?" The payoff is that you're angry. You're resentful. You're stuck. You're disappointed. You feel less than. You get to be a victim. You can justify why you aren't successful.

Perhaps you experienced an emotional or physical trauma. If you blame yourself for that which you had no control over, then you will continue to attract situations to fulfill those feelings. Instead of focusing on what happened to you, what can that event do for you today? It can allow you to be the person that you are destined to be. An adverse situation can be a huge part of your story, one that can impact and inspire others.

Connect the Dots

Take a look at some of your past events and see if you can connect the dots about why you procrastinate. For instance, many people procrastinate because they have anxiety about saying the wrong thing. What is the underlying emotional cause? A lot of times, it has something to do with our parents, or perhaps one of our teachers. Maybe it was someone down the street who lectured us, judged us, beat us up, traumatized us, or made fun of us. Therefore, we have anxiety about the words we say. Instead of making a mistake, we temper our words or say nothing at all. I've written about this in two of my previous books, *More Heart Than Talent* and *Psychologically Unemployable*, because I, too, have been a victim. I spent many years of my life living in my head, trying to overcome all the events that happened to me.

Reasons to Succeed

Create some reasons to succeed, reasons to let go of procrastination, reasons to let go of denial, reasons to become a six-figure income earner or a seven-figure income earner, reasons to become a person of influence, reasons to become a recovering procrastinator. These reasons require some clarity; just saying, "Freedom – I want freedom" is not enough. Your reasons must have some passion, some energy, some juice, and some vigor. You want others to feel that in you. Because if they sense your scarcity, your lack, or your poverty consciousness instead, they will do everything in their power to get away from you. People are attracted to people of influence and affluence. They want to be around people with joy and peace, people with integrity, people whose word means something. This requires a daily method of operation, clearly defined goals, and a game plan.

Become Conscious of Your Words and Actions

Create affirmations for yourself that describe who you are and who you are becoming, now that you are a recovering procrastinator.

"I am the leader people are looking for."

"I am letting go of procrastination one day at a time."

"I will isolate my procrastination to the cause that creates the effect."

"I am no longer procrastinating."

"I am letting go of my procrastination."

"Procrastination is no longer my identity."

Words are the beginning, but actions must follow. Learn to break time down into increments. It's advantageous to write a few things down, to have a daily method you operate in. It doesn't have to be complicated or overly regimented, but there has to be some order in the chaos. Become completion-conscious, decision-conscious. Become production-oriented.

Most procrastinators are quitters. Most procrastinators do not finish projects. They might start, but they dabble. They get ready to get ready. As a recovering procrastinator, you can develop the ability to delegate to yourself. Develop the ability to isolate problems and live in solutions. One example is to commit to completing your tax returns on time this year. Become time-conscious.

Develop a New Identity

Now, take a deep breath. Begin to see yourself as a producer, a highly productive entrepreneur, a highly productive salesperson, a highly productive person, a soul having a human experience, a person who experiences peace and joy.

You are a person who completes what they set out to accomplish. You are a person other people can count on, but they don't use you – they reward you. You have become a person of influence who others see as a mentor, a producer, someone who is no longer a procrastinator. You're a writer, a speaker. You're a leader of women and men. You're leading children. You are a leader, and now you're growing leaders. You are no longer a procrastinator. It's not your identity anymore.

You now live in a place that has very little clutter. You not only can get your cars in the garage, you have multiple cars in multiple garages. You have a hangar for your airplane and your helicopter. You have many zip codes that you reside in because you are a recovering procrastinator.

You are a producer, and your habits are based on solutions and production. People see you as a transformational expert. When you look in the mirror, you no longer see yourself as a loser. You no longer see yourself as a procrastinator. You no longer see yourself as someone who just can't get it done. Instead of sleeping in, you get up early, and you feel invigorated rather than exhausted. You are someone who accomplishes your goals. You have become a goal-getter.

As you learn to let go, you are offended less often. You are not easily hurt. People don't upset you. You don't fly off the handle. You don't resent people the way you used to. You have now learned to let others be right so you can be rich. You don't hold onto situations. You don't validate and justify. You live in the present.

How can you accomplish all of this? You begin. You begin right now. You start to break down your areas of procrastination, and you decide that in small increments that you will become achievement-oriented.

You don't set such big goals that you have a reason to procrastinate. I see this so often.

"What is your financial goal for this year?"

"Five hundred thousand."

"That's great. Have you ever made $1,000 as an entrepreneur?"

"Well, no."

Don't set such big goals that you can't possibly begin. Set smaller goals. A key word that must enter your vocabulary is "consistency." "I consistently produce." "I am consistent." "I am methodical."

Develop great habits, not just in production, but great habits when it comes to relaxation, great habits when it comes to diet, great habits when it comes to rest. Success is balance.

Key Areas of Change

We've looked at the six procrastination types. Now, as you learn to drop your procrastination, let's look at the six key areas of change: addictions, clutter, engaging in a new enterprise, health and fitness, relationships, and spirituality.

1. Addictions

"I promise I'm going to quit." "I promise I'm going to go on a diet." "I promise I'm going to stop smoking." "I promise I'm going to stop overeating." "I'm definitely going to pay off my credit cards. I'm going to do it today." "Well, I can't today; I'm busy. I'll definitely do it tomorrow." This is the language of addiction.

Addictions end up manifesting physically, but all addictions begin emotionally. What addictions do you have that keep you doing the same thing over and over, living in denial, living in poverty consciousness? What addictions keep you stuck?

_____

_____

_____

_____

_____

_____

_____

2. Clutter

Do you have a lot of clutter? Is your desk, your garage, or your closet overflowing? How about your bookkeeping, your accounting? Are you organized? Are many areas of your life a cluster of clutter? Is your house a maze of clutter? Do you take on so much that you can't possibly begin? Create a brief list of three situations in your life where your clutter no longer serves you. Next to each situation, choose a date to address the situation. Take a deep breath and approach this exercise without judgment or negativity. This is how you begin creating a window to look into your soul as a recovering procrastinator.

_____

_____

_____

_____

_____

_____

_____

3. Engaging in a New Enterprise

Do you have challenges selling, closing, following up, following through, developing a team, and marketing? Even though you might be dreaming of success in a new enterprise, what you are communicating is, "I am a noble struggler. I am a struggleaholic." Instead of focusing on all of the areas where you require improvement, use this time to acknowledge what you already do well. "I am good at _____. My strengths are _____." Great!

Now how can these skills and strengths be incorporated into your enterprise? You have a lifetime of development in front of you! Great producers use their strengths to create results while developing the areas of their lives that require attention and improvement.

_____

_____

_____

_____

_____

_____

4. Health and Fitness

Take a look at your physique. Are you living in the body you deserve to live in? Are you carrying extra weight? If you are, that's exhausting. Imagine wearing a belt with two gallons of water attached to it all day – how would that extra weight impede your progress? What does the extra weight represent? What emotions are you carrying around from past events that no longer serve you? What will you let go of today so you can carry a lighter emotional and physical load? You have lofty dreams, don't you? You deserve the emotional and physical body that will serve you in achieving those dreams. Not sure where to start? Contact me and I will connect you to some great resources to assist you in your transformation!

_____

_____

_____

_____

5. Relationships

Do you have challenges with intimacy because you're angry, or because you don't think you deserve it? Are you resentful? Do you have feelings of hate because of past abandonment? Do you have challenges with relationships because you feel like you're not good enough, or because you've been violated, hurt, neglected, or abused?

Do you have challenges devoting time to your intimate relationships? Do you procrastinate about taking vacations or taking time off? Are you so productive that you can't take time for dinner? Is all your time devoted to success to the point that there's no time for romance?

I have found in my journey that the true riches have been in the relationships I have forged and developed over time. Live this next year in a way that you will be proud of when you are eighty, ninety, or 100; learn to celebrate the joy of living as well as the joy of accomplishment.

_____

_____

_____

_____

_____

_____

6. *Spirituality*

How about your relationship with yourself? With God? Do you take time to meditate? Do you have any alone time? Do you get a restful night's sleep? Do you have spiritual beliefs? Do you understand the universal laws? You spirit requires at least as much attention as your bank account. In fact, for many of us, our bank account becomes a reflection of our spiritual self. Invest some energy each day in becoming the person you would seek as a mentor. You will find that when you are willing to follow your own footsteps in the journey of life, others are naturally attracted to you.

_____

_____

_____

_____

_____

Become a Student of Personal Development

If you're determined to change, you must become a student of change. Begin to understand the value of personal development and self-improvement. Stop giving lip service to it. Stop skimming the books, and start to put what you read into practical application. You can't just look at a book and get the content by osmosis.

I recently told my wife that when I started my first twelve-step program, I knew nothing about personal development. She looked at me in shock, and said, *"You?* You, Mr. Personal Development, knew nothing about it?" I didn't begin my spiritual journey until I was thirty-two years old. In my early twenties, I purchased the book *How to Master the Art of Selling* by Tom Hopkins. I scanned it and memorized it because my sales manager was going to give me a test on it. I put it down after that and never really read it.

The great Louise Hay's book, *You Can Heal Your Life*, was recommended to me in 1988, but once again, I never read it. It collected dust on my shelf for years. I was then given a gift, *The Road Less Traveled* by Scott Peck. Next, I bought my first Tony Robbins book. After that, I had the opportunity to see Jim Rohn, the father of personal development and self-improvement. I feel blessed to have shared the stage with him on five occasions, and I booked him to speak at four of my events.

If I had procrastinated about meeting Jim Rohn, I would never be the person that I am today. There was a moment when I said to myself, "Ah, he'll never shake my hand. I'll never be able to get through this crowd." However, winners always find a way, and a sense of purpose greater than self, called God, came over me and I was able to get my picture taken with the great Jim Rohn. That was a big turning point in my life, because that day I said, "Someday, I'm going to share the stage with Jim Rohn." That event took place fifteen years after I said this.

You see, dreams can come true, but you have to believe in the beauty of your dreams. You have to get in the game. You have to play the game. You have to let go of procrastination. You don't have to be productive 99 percent of the time – if you can be productive somewhere between 50 to 85 percent, your transformation will begin.

Give yourself a pat on the back. Give yourself a hand up rather than waiting for someone to give you a handout. There's always a hand up – that hand is called the hand of God, and he is always there when you are ready. But if you're not ready, then how can he ever acknowledge you? You must be able to step into that presence. You have to let go of situations that no longer serve you. You have all the skills, all the talent – you have everything you require.

"Patience" is one of the greatest words you can include in your vocabulary. If you don't have patience, develop it. You can't buy it, and you can't borrow it. It's something you become. In the process, you'll develop your unique story. But you won't be able to tell your story if you procrastinate. You want to share your story of victory, your story of overcoming the challenges, your story of overcoming the odds. People love stories. How about the story of a single mother, with three small kids, who didn't buy into her excuses, or the story of someone who is so strapped in debt that, instead of doing what everyone else does and filing bankruptcy, had the guts, the courage, and the intestinal fortitude to step to the plate and pay off $250,000 of unsecured debt? These stories have significance – they have meaning.

If you continue to procrastinate, you'll just be another victim tiptoeing quietly through life, living with the pain of regret, and arriving at your grave safely. You deserve to live the good life, and living the good life requires passion, dignity, and clarity.

Courage is a quality that never goes out of fashion; there is always a market for it. In addition, you must be inspired, not merely motivated. Come Monday morning, you'd better be inspired. This requires having reasons bigger than your problems. Nothing will overcome procrastination like having a dream. Nothing will overcome procrastination like finding a purpose bigger than yourself.

Let me explain something: Purpose doesn't always have to mean your life purpose. Purpose can be a daily purpose. Purpose doesn't have to be some bigger-than-life philanthropic purpose, where you're going to change the world. When you make a business call, what is the purpose of the call? I always say, "My name is Jeffery Combs. I received your name and number from _____," and I state the purpose of my call. You see, I have a purpose. If you don't have a purpose, you'll end up fulfilling someone else's purpose in a career called a job. Trading time for dollars will never get you to your Promised Land.

Live the Spirit of Free Enterprise

The spirit of free enterprise is why you picked up this book. You know in your heart of hearts that you're an entrepreneur. You know that there are no limits in free enterprise except the limits you place upon yourself. As you learn to let go of your limiting thoughts, you step into the "no limitations zone." When you are in that space, there is no procrastination because you are living life the way life was meant to be lived – loving people, loving God, loving what you do, and most importantly, loving yourself. I call these "The Four Ls." When you are living the four Ls, you don't have time to procrastinate. You have goals and objectives, so you don't procrastinate, because it costs you too much money. The reason I never get sick is because I can't afford it. The reason that I'm seldom a victim is that I spent too much of my life that way.

Take a look at how much time you have devoted to procrastinating. Isn't it time you got on with it? Isn't it time you got in the game? Isn't it time you developed your purpose? Isn't it time that you become the person you've always deserved to be? Isn't it time for you to live the good life? Isn't it time to let go? Isn't it time to become productive? It's time, because today you are a recovering procrastinator.

NOTES

9
THE SEVEN HABITS OF RECOVERING PROCRASTINATORS

I have developed seven habits that will allow you to live in the present, be much more productive, and eliminate the procrastination which no longer serves you.

Habit #1 – Manage Yourself in Time

This first habit involves working with time frames. To become a recovering procrastinator requires developing a much greater sense of time – one hour, one day, one week, one month, one quarter, one year. This is breaking time down into manageable time frames.

If you have a full time occupation, if you have a family, if you have a significant other, if you have pets, if you have spiritual obligations, if you have children, there's a high probability that you are overwhelmed. And if you are overwhelmed emotionally, there's a high probability that it will show up as procrastination. To eliminate being overwhelmed, it's important you understand what causes it.

The cause of overwhelm that creates the effect of procrastination is a multilayered subject, but in general, the reason most of us get overwhelmed is that our body goes into fight or flight. You have to choose to live in the solution, not the problem. There is chaos in the world, and the world will gladly volunteer to drag you into it. You have to create order in increments of time.

The concept of "time management" is a misnomer. What is important is that you master your emotions. You want to be able to manage yourself in frames of time.

You want to live much more in the present, without being so rigid about time. You don't want to have to always look at time. Make time your ally, not your enemy.

The Power of Fifteen Minutes

Here's a very simple way to change your whole perspective of time: Break time down into fifteen-minute increments. Begin to practice this; see what you can accomplish in fifteen minutes. Take an area of your life where there is a lot of clutter. The clutter represents being overwhelmed. (FYI, if you're overwhelmed, there's a high probability that you're underpaid. There is a direct correlation between being overwhelmed and under-received, or under-prosperous.)

In fifteen minutes, if you are effective, you can accomplish a lot. Whether it's a closet, a workbench, a desk, a refrigerator, or a cabinet, take a deep breath, get a thirty-three-gallon trash bag, and throw away everything you possibly can throw away in those fifteen minutes. Organize everything you can possibly organize in those fifteen minutes.

Make sure you don't do this frantically, because then you'll be overwhelmed in your overwhelm. As you do this exercise, do your best not to let the old voice of the past interject and interrupt your present by saying, "Oh, this is so big. What's the use? I'll never get it all cleaned up."

Do you realize that, during a sporting event, an entire game can change in the last quarter? Teams have actually overcome twenty-point deficits and more in a single quarter of a game – fifteen minutes of measured time. Fifteen minutes is a long time when measured, evaluated, and turned into productive energy.

The next step is to take one hour. What can you accomplish in one hour? Look at the garage. Look at what a disaster it is. Look at your taxes. Look at your drawer. Look at a closet. Look at any situation where you feel overwhelmed.

Typically, when you go into overwhelm, your shoulders hunch up and your neck sinks down into your body. You grind your teeth; you shut down, melt down, lie down – quite frankly, you *are* down because you have no self-esteem. Being overwhelmed is a very helpless feeling, and to overcome this situation, you learn to break time down into realistic increments that measure production.

If you want to achieve more, you must become more. Your self-talk will either lead you to prosperity or lead you to poverty – you decide. One will reward you, and one will end in regret. Which one will you choose? The answer is obvious. To become a recovering procrastinator, you will value time differently.

Every day, when your eyes flutter open, you are granted a new gift called time – twenty-four hours, 86, 400 seconds. Imagine that you received $86,400 every single day, and you were required to use every penny of it, spend it, contribute it, give it to charity, enjoy it – but you wouldn't get any of it back. You would probably get bored with it at some point, but in reality, it would be a lot of fun to give it your best effort.

So, when it comes to time, change your perspective. Begin to value time. Borrow time from areas that don't serve you.

Become a multitasker, a multi-doer – a highly productive soul having a productive human experience.

Habit #2 – Set Small Goals; Take Small Steps One Day at a Time

It's very common for procrastinators to set huge goals. They're going to have a half-million-dollar year in their first year as a business owner. They're going to go from high-school actor to winning an Oscar. Instead, what typically happens is that they implode emotionally because they get overwhelmed. Those overwhelmed feelings create guilt and shame, resentment, and disappointment that deplete the emotional energy required to move forward toward a goal.

When it comes to goal setting, the real value in a goal is getting it. The goals you get are the goals you accomplish. The goals that you give yourself permission to enjoy are the ones that give you a sense of purpose, a sense of pride.

The goals that most people don't get are the ones that lead to regret. "I'll go ahead and set the goal, but these things usually don't happen to me." "Yeah, I'll give it a shot; I'll try." "I hope it works out." With that kind of attitude, you might as well pack it in before you even begin. If you don't have a clearly defined goal, if it's vague, there's a high probability that you will never achieve it.

Certain goals must be spiritual. When you have that kind of feeling, that internal inspiration, and that kind of connection, you will not be denied. However, instead of setting big, lofty goals, think "realistic" – think "objective." Plan to accomplish your goals; plan to achieve them. Don't leave any margin for major error when you set a goal. That's why my advice is not to set a goal so big that you can't possibly achieve it, because then all you've done is set yourself up for disappointment... and procrastination.

Many speakers, authors, and writers have their own variation of goal-setting. Here's my version: "Don't set so many goals that you lose sight of the most important ones." I've heard speakers say, "Write 100 goals down on a piece of paper, and when you accomplish your first 100, write another 100." Now, there's merit to an exercise like this, but in reality, a large percentage of the population can't even come up with 100 goals, and they seldom achieve the ones they do write down because they're addicted to disappointment.

Disappointment always leads to some level of procrastination. Procrastination allows us to feel bad, which leads to more disappointment – hence, the term "addicted to a feeling." Accomplishing goals requires you to be realistic.

One of my clients, who is in a direct-sales business, set a goal of enrolling thirty people in a calendar month. Now, that would be a stretch for a superstar, but for her, even though she was a bright, articulate woman, the odds were slim to none. Prior to setting this goal, she had never signed up more than a couple of people or closed more than a couple of sales in a calendar month.

I asked her what inspired her to set such a big goal. "Well, I see everyone else in my circle of influence creating these giant numbers. If I can't create those kind of numbers, then I'm just a loser."

I said, "Actually, you're not a loser. First of all, don't ever compare yourself to someone else when it comes to setting a goal. You have no idea what someone else has been through. You have no idea of their skills, their habits, or their mindset. In addition, just because someone has created a *result* doesn't mean that they're going to continue to create *results*."

Many people that have achieved big accomplishments also have experienced big disasters, big sabotages, and big failures. Don't compare yourself to other people –it's not fair to you, and it's not fair to them. Acknowledge others, endorse them, be proud of them – but don't feel resentful because they're achieving something that you're not. If you use this as an excuse to procrastinate, living the law of entitlement and feeling that you're entitled to success without going through the process, then once again all you're doing is setting yourself up for failure and disappointment.

Set small goals. If your goal is to become a millionaire, before you ever become a millionaire, first you have to stop sucking air. The reality is that you'll either suck air or become a millionaire; you decide. But to become a millionaire, you must develop the habits of a millionaire. The habits of a millionaire require you to be highly productive in the hours you devote to producing results. This is why small goals are a great way to build a solid foundation.

When you reach a goal, reward yourself. We'll cover this in detail in step number six, but as it relates to achieving goals, no matter how small, when you accomplish a goal, pat yourself on the heart. Say, "I am enough. I am capable." Give yourself some credit for what you accomplish. Don't judge yourself.

While it's important to write your goals down, it's essential to have a vision of their outcome. When you set a goal, what you're really doing is describing the outcome. Make sure that you create some passion and meaning around your goal. If you don't, it will be just another ho-hum goal. Since you'll most likely have to overcome obstacles, challenges, emotional brick walls, and possible opposition from family members, energy, passion, and vision are crucial.

Habit #3 – Perform the Task Itself

As a recovering procrastinator, you've become a student of personal development, self-improvement, and self-empowerment. You are a student of entrepreneurship. Become a student of your vocation; become a student of your emotions. Have a good idea of what you are getting paid for. Be clear about the task at hand. Keep your clearly defined goal in front of you as you focus on the next actions that will bring you closer to its accomplishment.

It's very effective to break each task down. This may be on paper, or it may be just a thought process. The task itself is the solution, and to live in the solution, you must understand the components of the goal. You must understand the vocation that you're operating in. Most people when they're relatively new at entrepreneurship don't really understand that they get paid for results only. Not understanding the industry or their role as an entrepreneur, they procrastinate and spend their time getting ready to get ready.

A ninety-day game plan with clearly articulated goals and a daily method of operation defines the individual tasks along the way. You want to take calculated risks; you want to have a strategy.

Habit #4 – Write Things Down

Especially if you are prone to procrastinate, keeping an organized list assists you to develop much more clarity. Way too many people operate like a spinning top, scattered in all directions. They end up being late for meetings. They're late for the airport. They forget appointments. They can't find their cell phone with all their contacts, they forget to pay a bill, or they experience a multitude of other situations because of their disorganization. Being organized is a skill. If you're not organized, there's a high probability that you are rebelling against your own success and on your way to becoming a rebellious rebel.

Getting organized means keeping lists. You might use a Day-Timer, or you might prefer to keep your lists and appointments online. You can use a BlackBerry or an iPhone, but whatever you do, get organized. You can't operate on a scrap of paper. You have to have a method.

I use a very simple At-a-Glance® black spiral book that I can pick up at any office supply store every year. I have a stack of them going back all the way to 1998. I break my time down by the hour. I get up at a certain time every single day; I am a creature of habit. Many people ask, "Isn't that boring?" Usually that person is broke or broken and is not a creature of routines.

To become successful in any endeavor, you must understand success principles. You must live the laws of success. You must develop habits, routines, skills, and a mindset that will allow you to succeed in the particular vocation that you have chosen. If you don't, you set yourself up to become a procrastinator.

The Seven Habits of Recovering Procrastinators

Many of my clients call me to tell me they have forgotten our coaching appointment, or their computer crashed, or they have lost their BlackBerry. Fortunately for them, I am organized. I have all of my coaching clients organized in my calendar. I am low-tech, big-check. I'm one of those old-school kind of guys. I still like good old-fashioned legal pads and Cross pens. I love black ink on yellow paper. This might not be your niche, but you have to find a way to be organized. Writing everything down is one way. You'll begin to live off your list. Create a system to keep your daily lists.

I update my list before I go to bed. I put it right on the corner of my desk. When I get up, it's available. I leave my assistant a series of voicemails at the end of the evening from my list; this eliminates a lot of chaos, instead of letting him just wing it. I do this so he can be organized. Since he's already an organized person, this is when organization meets organization.

You should be proud of being organized. If you are addicted to procrastination, this is definitely a situation that you deserve to release. If you're a recovering procrastinator, there's a high probability that you were, at one point in your life, a caretaker of some sort. It's very common for a caretaker to get overwhelmed. They don't keep their time frames properly. They do too much for others and find themselves overwhelmed, resentful that they don't have a life.

Begin to affirm: "I am organized. Organizing my life is easy." The way you live and the way you operate usually are in direct proportion to the person you have become.

Habit #5 – Eliminate Distractions

Distractions are what keep us in procrastination mode. "You don't have any idea of what's like – I'm homeschooling my children," I've had clients tell me. They're right; I've never had children. However, I have a pretty good idea of what it's like to be distracted. Many parents use their kids as an excuse to stay distracted. They don't discipline themselves. They don't discipline their children. They let them walk in and out of their office anytime, and that's no way to run an enterprise.

If you have a lot of distractions in your life, there's a high probability that a huge percentage of your most valuable commodity – time – is being borrowed, stripped away, or taken from you. If you don't eliminate distractions, the distractions actually end up becoming your identity.

What are some of the main distractions that affect us? We process. We're not really present in a conversation. We're looking out the window. We pay attention to every situation that's required except the task at hand.

The words we use keep us distracted, "Uh, huh." "Yeah…" "Okay." "Sure." The most powerful word in the English language when it comes to transformation is "yes." Get comfortable saying, "Yes." Saying "yes" will assist you to eliminate a lot of distractions.

Do you deserve to let go of that clutter? "Yes!" Are you going to your company's convention this year? "Well, if something doesn't get in the way, I'll be there." Um, I'll give it a shot." "Okay, I'll try." So many of us let life get in the way.

If this is true of you, time is your enemy rather than your ally.

Spending excessive amounts of time online is a major distraction. Facebook and Twitter have become huge distractions for a large percentage of the population, both men and women. While social media is important, you don't want to be distracted by it when you are producing. If you let that take you out of your rhythm, you'll have a challenge getting back into it.

Eliminating distractions will give you a direct experience of the words "letting go." When you let go of distractions, you're in the present. You're in the moment. You unequivocally, absolutely deserve to receive, and you're in the place to do so.

Distractions rob you of your energy because they rob you of your focus. It's your responsibility to stay in the present and eliminate as many distractions as you possibly can. When you decide to change, it's amazing, because a lot of the people in your circle of influence sense it. They may not know exactly what it means, but they definitely feel it and respond accordingly. On the other hand, if you let distractions become your identity, what you've created tells others, "I am distractible."

Eliminating distractions is a commitment. It is a decision. And it's absolutely, unequivocally a skill you require to master because if you don't, you will let the wind blow, and all of a sudden you will be off course. You have to have bounce-back ability. You have to have guts, willpower. You have to have an attitude. You have to feel comfortable about who you are and what you're becoming, so that you can eliminate the distractions.

Habit # 6 – Become Reward-Conscious

Become reward-conscious – this means ABR: Always Be Receiving. We are so conditioned to give that we end up having challenges receiving. Receiving is a skill that absolutely enhances your people skills when it comes to marketing and selling. To be able to connect with others and close sales, you first must find some good people. Once you find them, you must develop and/or attract them.

The reward is the payoff. The reward is what you get for the risk. If you never take a risk, there's seldom, if ever, a reward. Learn to become reward conscious. Reward is what you envision in the future. The reason you go for the reward is so that you have goals and objectives bigger than your problems. In addition to becoming reward-conscious, learn to become production-conscious.

Focus on results. If you are reward-conscious, you will absolutely be rewarded. Most of life is a contact sport. It's a nonphysical sport, but many contacts have to be created. You have to learn to converse with people, ask them questions, show them products and services, and deliver value. You must be able to get paid, because if you don't, you will end up with a nonprofit organization from the discomfort of your home.

If the reward is big enough, and you're passionate enough about it, there's a high probability that you will overcome your procrastination to receive it that reward. And you absolutely deserve to receive the reward!

THE SEVEN HABITS OF RECOVERING PROCRASTINATORS

Habit #7 – Learn the Skill of Self-Evaluation

The last step in becoming a highly effective recovering procrastinator is self-evaluation. Self-evaluation means that you are a student, a lifelong learner. You can offend someone, you can make a mistake, you can sabotage yourself, but with self-evaluation, you can take a look at the whole picture. You can look at situations objectively.

You can forgive yourself. You can ask forgiveness of others. You have some humility, some dignity, and you're able to look at situations for what they are, instead of what they aren't. You're able to be comfortable with the process. In the middle of a feeling, you can take a deep breath and not collapse. You spend less time being overwhelmed. You're able to see a situation and, rather than engage it, you can walk away from it. You don't have to argue for the sake of arguing. When you're able to evaluate yourself, you can, with humility, admit when you created a mistake without judging yourself.

Self-evaluation gives you bounce-back ability, which allows you to stay in the game. Without self-evaluation, there's a high probability that you will blame others. You will point the finger at someone else.

Self-evaluation enables you to be objective. Being objective is absolutely a reward. Being objective will allow you to evaluate a situation for what it is rather than blaming someone for what it isn't. This kind of insight allows you to become a recovering procrastinator.

If you're not honest, you will live in denial. A pathological liar is someone who actually believes his or her own lies. Many individuals lie to themselves about procrastination. They may admit to procrastinating, but they refuse to look at the cause that creates the effect. To move out of denial and live in awareness is a liberating experience because it opens you up to a higher level of consciousness. Self-evaluation is the key. Anger, hate, guilt, resentment, abandonment, rejection, feelings of being overwhelmed – which one of these emotions has the greatest effect on you?

Self-evaluation allows you to understand the cause that creates the effect. Self-evaluation is liberating; denial is intoxicating. Being a producer will reward you. Being a procrastinator leads to living life full of regret.

These seven steps of the highly effective recovering procrastinator are the foundation of your journey from chronically procrastinating to producing the results that will set you free in life. First, manage yourself in time. Realize that time does not get away from you; you lose yourself in situations that distract you and shift your attention and focus away from your goal. Begin to allot small increments of time where you commit to one task at hand, and be committed to completing that task within the time you have set aside.

Second, set small goals that you can accomplish in one day, one week, one month, or one quarter.

Third, practice performing the actions that will move you toward accomplishing the goals you have set. Setting goals is easy; getting goals can also be easy, but you may require a shift in perspective and a shift in your habits for this transformation.

Fourth, keep an organized list of your objectives and responsibilities. Mark items as completed and reward yourself for a job well done.

Fifth, do your best to eliminate distractions from your productive time. This may require disciplining both yourself and those around you as you change your habits.

Sixth, reward yourself for every stride forward that you take, no matter how big or small it may seem at the time. Change is progressive, and you have the courage to embark on the journey. You deserve credit – give credit where credit is due!

Finally, be objective as you evaluate your progress. Perfect transformation is an imaginary pressure we put on ourselves. You will probably create some mistakes or slip back into old habit patterns as you strive for change. Objective self-evaluation will allow you to move very quickly back into the space where you are in alignment with the goals you have set, the contracts you have created with yourself and others, and keep you moving forward toward becoming the productive, peaceful person you were born to be.

NOTES

10
THE PROCRASTINATOR QUIZ

This last chapter will provide you with a series of forty true or false questions to assist you in identifying your current level of procrastination, as well as give you a clear understanding of what steps are necessary in executing your recovery plan. Take this quiz while you're in a relaxed environment where you can contemplate and answer the questions objectively. At the end of the questionnaire, you'll be able to evaluate whether you're a procrastinator or a producer, and you'll be able to determine if your procrastination borders on being chronic, or if you're a moderate procrastinator. Are you ready?

The Procrastinator Quiz

1. I return phone calls promptly.

Does it take you a long time to get back to people, or do you do return phone calls promptly? Do you let your phone calls pile up in your voice mail, taking several days to get back to them? Or perhaps you don't ever get back to them at all. If you're really in the game, you're the kind of person that returns all phone calls promptly.

2. I create decisions quickly and promptly.

Do you pontificate, hesitate, levitate, or meditate when it comes to deciding? Do you agonize over your decisions? Do you ask other people for insight on decisions you're about to make, or do you decide quickly? Do you promptly let go of the decisions you create, or do you agonize over your decisions? Do you doubt and undoubt, do and undo the decisions you make? Do you toss and turn because of what you did or didn't decide?

3. I never incur late fees for credit cards or overdue bills.

Do you pay credit card bills on time, or do you let your statements stack up in a drawer until it's overwhelming? Do you pay the minimum due on your credit card statement, incurring interest fees? Are you charged late fees for past due bills? Are your finances organized so that you are aware of when a bill is due?

4. I do my Christmas and birthday shopping promptly and ahead of time.

Do you wait until the last minute to buy gifts, or do you plan ahead for upcoming events? Do you operate in crisis mode? Do you send Christmas cards after Christmas? Do you send belated birthday cards, or do you miss birthdays altogether?

5. When I dine, I do my dishes quickly, not letting them pile up in the sink.

Do you clean up after yourself, or do you allow dirty dishes to stack up in the sink and overflow onto the counters? Do you dry your dishes and put them away immediately, or do you let your dishes air dry in the sink, leaving them there until the next time you use them?

6. I don't delay starting on projects I have to do.

Do you put off your honey-do projects until they become honey-I -don't-dos? Do you wait until the weekend, the end of the month, the end of the quarter, the end of six months, or the end of the year – or until you can no longer get your car in the garage? Do you have good intentions at the beginning of a Saturday and then suddenly find that you've procrastinated the day away? Or do you go out and start a project, completing it so you can take the rest of the day off?

7. I pay my bills as soon as they arrive.

Do you pay your bills right away when they arrive? If you're like me, do you pay the bills the very day you get them, even putting the stamp on the envelope? Do you allow your bills to compound? Do they pile up? Do you forget about them? Do you stuff them in a drawer? Do you lose them? Do you have a system for paying your bills, or do you wait until the very last minute when you're in chronic crisis mode?

8. I don't miss concerts and sporting events because I remember to buy tickets ahead of time.

Do you wait until the last minute to buy tickets for concerts or sporting events, only to be disappointed because all the good seats are already taken? Or you purchase them ahead of time, getting the best prices, the best value, and the best seats?

9. When there are recurring tasks that I should be doing (i.e., prospecting, marketing, general business tasks, etc.), I don't avoid them because of perceived pain.

Are you able to set a time, jump right in, and enjoy what you do? Or do you spend time avoiding the pain, inventing reasons to put off what you perceive as unpleasant? Do you go ahead and do what you say you're going to do?

10. I set regular dental checkups and medical appointments and I keep these appointments.

Do you avoid the dentist because of perceived pain, putting off regular checkups until you really are in pain? Do you get regular physical checkups, following through with tests and blood work your physician recommends? Are you proactive about your health, or do you operate in denial?

11. When I travel, I'm at the airport well in advance. I'm never late and I never miss my flights because I'm very conscientious about being at the airport on time.

Are you on time for your flight, or do you create adrenaline by frantically rushing? Do you arrive at the airport at the last minute? When there is a long line for security, do you fidget, worrying that you're not going to make your flight? Do you absolutely have to run to the gate? Have you ever been the last one on the plane, not because the plane has been delayed but because you have been delayed? Or are you prompt, conscientious, on time, and relaxed when you arrive at the airport?

12. I'm able to park my vehicle in my garage comfortably without a lot of clutter.

Do you have floor-to-ceiling clutter? Do one or more of your cars have to sit outside your garage because your garage is full of stuff?

13. My workspace is neat and orderly; it's a very comfortable place from which to produce results.

Is your desk clean and tidy, or is it an absolute disaster? Is your office in chaos? Would you be proud to let someone see your desk? Or are you embarrassed to have anyone in your office?

14. I make lists, completing and crossing off items in a timely, relaxed, precise manner.

Do you write down a list of what you intend to accomplish on a daily basis? Or do you resist making lists? Are you out of control? Do you forget what you're supposed to be doing? Do you end up being late, missing appointments, and relying on others to remind you?

15. I am good about organizing my errands, and I create as few trips as possible.

Do you run around like a chicken with its head cut off? Or do you efficiently plan your errands? Are you constantly going back and forth, picking up items that you forgot, or are you thorough and organized with a routine and a system?

16. I answer questions quickly without having to think about the answer.

Do you answer questions decisively, or do you hem and haw until you can come up with an answer? Are you a person who can answer a question directly, or are you a person who tells a story?

17. I seldom repeat a question when someone asks me one.

Have you trained yourself not to repeat a question? Or do you repeat the question someone asks you so you can stop and think about how to answer perfectly? Can you receive a question and then just state the answer, or do you have to think about it, repeat it, and take three to eight seconds to answer?

18. I seldom say "um" when answering a question or starting a sentence.

"Um" is not a word; "um" is a sound. Do you fall into the habit of using this sound to buy yourself time, or are you decisive and congruent enough to drop this sound from your vocabulary?

19. I'm detailed and prepared when I shop, and I seldom forget items.

Are you someone that goes to the grocery store without a list and then wonder why you spent $300 when you only intended to spend $100? Are you as unorganized in your shopping as you are in your garage or your closets? Do you look at prices and have any idea what you're buying, or do you just buy right off the shelf without any intuition? Do you carry a list when you shop? Do you only get the items on your list? When you arrive home, do you put away your purchases efficiently and professionally?

20. I am a thorough packer when I go on a business trip or a vacation.

Do you plan what to pack, or do you cram everything into your suitcase at the very last minute? Is your suitcase so full that you actually have to sit on it to zip it, and then when you get to the airport it weighs too much and you have to pay an extra fee? You may not realize it, but your suitcase represents your emotional state. Are you neat and thorough? Do you consider yourself to be an exceptional packer?

21. I do my laundry regularly; it never builds up, and I never fall behind.

Do you do your laundry only when you're out of clothes? Do you have stacks of clothes in your bedroom and in the laundry room? Do you require more than one laundry basket because it's overflowing? Or do you take a lot of pride in the way you hang and fold your clothes?

22. I am good at meeting deadlines and often complete tasks long before their deadlines.

Are you deadline-conscious? Do you finish projects way ahead of time? Do you have a plan, a method, and a routine? Or are you all over the map, always running behind schedule, receiving negative feedback for not being able to meet your deadlines?

23. My home is exceptionally neat, clean, and organized.

Is your house clean and organized, or is it a battle zone, a pigpen, and a recipe for disaster? Do you often misplace items or are unable to find important papers due to the clutter, or is your home clean, clutter-free, and calm?

24. I don't overstuff my closets.

Is it difficult for you to hang a garment because of how packed your closet is? Do you have boxes on top of boxes in the closet? Do you have piles of shoes stacked on top of each other? Are you ashamed of your closet, or are you proud of how neat and orderly it is?

26. When I go out for the evening, I seldom have to do something at the last minute.

Do you have to constantly call other people to take care of situations you forgot? Do you wait until the very last minute to get dressed? Are you trying to do two or three things at the same time, or do you calmly leave your house without any concerns about whether you turned the iron off or locked the door? Are you in a relaxed state or a frantic state when you leave the house?

27. I seldom get behind in my day-to-day tasks.

Do you have a method of operation? Do you have a daily routine, one that you stick to? Do you have simple habits that you perform consistently every single day? Are you a creature of habit? Do you get up at the same time each day? Or do you live haphazardly, with no sense of a daily plan?

28. I seldom feel overwhelmed emotionally.

Do you operate from a calm, relaxed state? Do you take life as it comes, or do you often get rattled? Do you try to control situations, or do you stay in the moment? Are you often angry, resentful, and overwhelmed? Do you cause drama and chaos? Are you all over the map, or are you right in the middle of the moment?

29. I usually keep my gas tank full; I rarely drive until the tank is almost empty.

Do you wait until the very last minute to get gas? Have you run out of gas more than two times in your life? Do you like to live on the edge of the edge because of the adrenaline rush it gives you? Or is your driving experience calm and pleasurable, with no unnecessary drama?

30. I take the garbage out frequently so it doesn't pile up.

Do you wait until your garbage is overflowing before you take it out, or do you take your trash out at least once a day? Does your trash smell because you empty it infrequently? Do you forget to put the trash out to get picked up, or do you make sure it's ready for the trash pickup the night before?

31. I am committed to an exercise routine at least three to four days a week.

Do you have a consistent exercise routine? Are you overweight? Do you stuff your feelings with food? Do you constantly tell yourself that you're going to get in shape, or that you're going to lose weight? Do you have a simple exercise routine that you follow regularly?

32. I don't let my email messages pile up.

Do you clean out your email inbox every couple of hours, or do you allow unread mail to accumulate to the point that you never get to it? Are your customer service skills exceptional? Do you have a system for filing emails you want to reference later? Or do you process emails in a random, unfocused way?

33. I'm good at answering emails and Facebook messages quickly.

Do you allow correspondence to accumulate to the point of overwhelm? Or do you systematically keep on top of messages, answering them quickly and efficiently? Do you waste time on social media sites, allowing yourself to become distracted? Or do you utilize social media in a way that enhances your goals and your life?

34. When the alarm goes off, I get up promptly, and I start my day fresh, alert, and ready to produce.

Do you stay in bed after your alarm goes off and then create excuses not to get up? Do you hit the snooze button more than once? Do you get up at a set time without an alarm clock? Do you wake up before the alarm even goes off? Do you forget to set the alarm, thus causing drama and chaos before the day has even really begun? Do you get to bed at a reasonable time each night so you can create a restful night's sleep, or do you habitually burn the candle at both ends?

35. When planning parties, events, seminars, etc., I do so well in advance.

Do you wait until the last minute to plan the details concerning events or parties? Do you find yourself frantically trying to book a hotel at the last minute? Do you often have to pay more because you're forced to – not because you choose to? Are you the type of person who always gets the best room, at the best hotel, at the best rate because you've done your homework and planned ahead?

36. I seldom let food spoil in the refrigerator; my refrigerator is organized and spotless.

Are you a packrat when it comes to your refrigerator? Is it so full of items that you can't find things easily? Do you buy more than you require at the grocery store and then find that you can't possibly use it? Are you a grocery store shopaholic? Does the food that you buy end up spoiling? Or do you keep a lightly but well-stocked refrigerator, one that's neat and clean? Do you regularly clean the shelves, the doors, and the bins? Are you proud of your refrigerator, or is it so crowded that you hate opening the door?

37. I set goals that are realistic and achievable, and I frequently accomplish them.

Do you set goals so big that you can't possibly achieve them? Do you set goals that are so overwhelming that you don't even start them? Do you create goals that just give you a reason to procrastinate, or do you set realistic, attainable goals that you are able to achieve, even if you have to stretch a little? Do you rashly set goals that you don't accomplish, or do you carefully set goals that you intend to achieve and then achieve them?

38. I take care of all necessary tasks before I relax and go to bed.

Are you good about planning your day the night before? Are you good about cleaning up before you go to bed? Do you perform routine tasks so you don't have to do them in the morning? Or do you fall into bed exhausted, leaving many routine things unfinished? Are you a multitasker or a multi-procrastinator?

39. I regularly balance my checkbook, and I have a good handle on my finances.

Do you neglect to enter checks in your checkbook register? Are you unaware of how much is in your checkbook? Are you out of money when you're out of checks? Is your bookkeeping in total chaos? Do you hand your accountant a box with unsorted receipts at the end of the year, or are your receipts categorized and organized? Do you use Quickbooks? Do you enter the data yourself, saving money at tax time?

40. I know my monthly financial overhead for both my business and personal expenses.

Are you aware of what money comes in and what goes out? Do you have a savings strategy for the next several years, or are you living from paycheck to paycheck? Do you have a household budget? Do you spend money without any idea of what you can afford? Do you frequently incur overdraft fees in your checking account? Do you plan time to map out a tax strategy for the upcoming years? Are you a wise steward with your money?

Your Procrastinator Score

Now that you've taken the procrastinator quiz, let's see where you really stand as a procrastinator. Remember, you only procrastinate in isolated areas that you perceive pain and/or rebel, so even though your score may not be favorable, keep in mind that you can break down any addiction and/or emotion one day at a time. To break any habit requires that you first begin to address the feelings that affect the cause.

To score the questionnaire, give yourself one point for each question you answered false and then total up the points.

24 or above: You are a chronic procrastinator, and procrastination keeps you stuck in many areas of your life.

14 to 23: Your procrastination borders on being chronic, and you require an overhaul session where you release as much clutter and procrastination as possible.

6 to 13: You are a moderate to average procrastinator who definitely requires some fine-tuning, but you're well on your way to becoming a recovering procrastinator.

5 or less: You are highly productive, and procrastination is a minor issue in your life. Even though it's minor, however, there's always room for improvement.

Remember, you'll never receive 100 percent on any score of this nature. Procrastination is an effect, not a cause. To become a recovering procrastinator, you must be aware of why you do what you do. Your focus must be on letting go of the areas where procrastination shows up in your life. Your goal is to become aware of the feelings that take you into procrastination. One way to begin is to take deep breaths from deep down in your diaphragm and even deeper into your groin so you can release the pain that keeps you doing the same thing over and over, stuck in procrastination.

Congratulations on reaching the end of this book. I celebrate the success you will create on your continuing journey of recovery from procrastination. You absolutely deserve to be free of the limitations procrastination has led to in your life –you deserve to have it all!

NOTES

NOTES

Jeffery Combs

Jeffery Combs, president of Golden Mastermind Seminars, Inc. is an internationally recognized speaker, trainer, and author, specializing in prospecting, leadership, personal breakthroughs, prosperity consciousness, spiritual enlightenment, mindset training, and effective marketing. His training revolves around personal growth and development, cuts to the chase, and delivers information that makes an immediate impact on your success!

Jeff is the author the author of numerous books, as well as motivational and personal development products, including the best-selling audio CD series, Confessions of a Recovering Procrastinator.

Jeff is available for consulting, mentoring, and personal one-on-one coaching. His professional guidance will assist you to create maximum results now!

For further information, please call 800-595-6632 or visit him online at www.GoldenMastermind.com.

NEW FROM JEFFERY COMBS!

7-Figure Connecting Secrets Revealed!

Are you ready to create 7-figure income results in your enterprise? Successful careers are launched and fueled by skillfully created connections and you will be amazed when you discover how easy connecting really is! In this CD Jeffery Combs shares the simple skills he uses over and over to create connections with people in life and in business to consistently achieve 7-figure income results.

1. Develop Opportunity Seeking Perception
2. Ask Quality Questions
3. Listen and Receive
4. Ask for Referrals
5. Use Your Network
6. Listen to Your Intuition
7. Attract Great Connectors

BECOME A RECOVERING PROCRASTINATOR

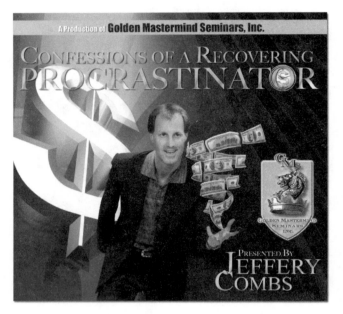

In this powerful 10-CD audio program, Jeff teaches you the skills to release the feelings that keep you procrastinating. You'll learn the skills he has developed and perfected to create multiple seven-figure income results so that you can be the person you deserve to be!

- To identify the cause of your procrastination
- How to neutralize the feeling of procrastination
- The six procastinator personality types
- The process of change
- How to go from procrastinator to producer
- How to let go of control

In addition, this program includes a
40 question procrastination quiz!

www.GoldenMastermind.com

More Heart Than Talent
by Jeffery Combs

"Listen to him, learn what he says and live his wise, brilliant advice.
It will make your life infinitely better."
- Mark Victor Hansen
The Power of Focus and Co-Creator of Chicken Soup for the Soul

This Book Will Assist You to:

- Step Out of Your Talent and Into Your Heart
- Become The Leader Other People Are Looking For
- Become a Goal Getter, Not a Goal Setter
- Develop an Agenda for Change
- Understand Why You Do What You Do
- Glide Through Adversity
- Manage Yourself Instead of Your Time
- Develop Your Emotional Resilience
- Get Off the Emotional Roller Coaster!
- Live in Your Intuition
- Feel From Your Heart
- Be In The Moment

"On the journey to success, heart beats talent every time!"
- Jeffery Combs

PSYCHOLOGICALLY UNEMPLOYABLE
LIFE ON YOUR TERMS

The Information In This Book Will Assist You To:

- Develop an Entrepreneurial Profile
- Turn Challenges Into Triumphs
- Get Money Right Emotionally
- Raise Your Deserve Quotient
- Master the Art of Listening
- Define Your Identity as an Entrepreneur
- Win the Game of Free Enterprise to Live Life on Your Terms!

The game of free enterprise and entrepreneurship is really the game of your life, and the question is: "Are you ready to play?" Are you ready to start? When the whistle blows, will you be ready to take off from the starting line, or will you be sitting on the bench tying your shoes? Are you ready to get in the game of free enterprise? If so, you are playing for high stakes – your freedom, your dreams and your life on your terms!

Now Available at
www.BarnesandNoble.com
www.Amazon.com

WOMEN IN POWER

A WOMAN'S GUIDE TO FREE ENTERPRISE

BY ERICA COMBS

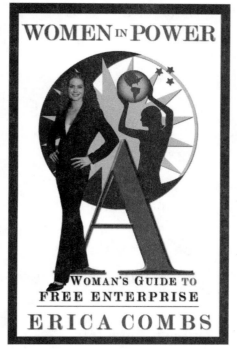

If you are ready to have free enterprise free you financially, emotionally and spiritually read my friend Erica's brilliant new book."

– Mark Victor Hansen
Co-creator, #1 New York Times best selling series
Chicken Soup for the Soul ®
Co-author, Cracking the Millionaire Code and The One
Minute Millionaire

Erica Combs is a woman who knows her power. Her creativity, talent and heart will assist you to achieve the success you seek.

- Jim Rohn
America's Foremost Business Philosopher

   Whether you are already a successful entrepreneur, just beginning a new venture or simply romancing the vision of owning your own business one day, this book will greatly assist you to understand how to win the game of free enterprise.

   Success will require that you begin to examine your current beliefs and give yourself permission to release those which no longer serve you so that you may adopt new and empowering beliefs to lead you to manifesting your dreams.

   The purpose of this book is to create a foundation for you to begin your journey to personal power, and to create an anchor you can use to reconnect with your internal peace as you continue your journey of personal development in the land of free enterprise!

www.GoldenMastermind.com

NOTES

NOTES

NOTES

NOTES

NOTES

NOTES